RECLAIMING OUR SCHOOLS:

Whose Kids Are They, Anyway?

RECLAIMING
OUR
SCHOOLS

Whose Kids Are They, Anyway?

Richard L. King, Ed. D

ELDERBERRY PRESS
Oakland, Oregon

For additional postpaid copies of this book,
send cover price to:
ELDERBERRY PRESS
1393 Old Homestead Road, Suite 1200
Oakland, Oregon 97462—9506

Publisher's Catalog-in-Publication Data
Reclaiming Our Schools:
 Whose Children Are They, Anyway?
 Richard L.King, Ed.D
 ISBN 0-9658407-9-4
1. Education.
2. School Reform.
3. Education Reform.
I. Title
This book was written, printed, and bound
in the United States of America
9 8 7 6 5 4 3 2 1

To Jack Shewmaker,
retired President of Wal-Mart Corporation,
as a representative of the many students
who taught me more about student learning
than any college or university course.
They taught me that students will perform up to
(or down to) the level teachers expect of them
and that students can hit any achievement target
they can see, and that stands still for them.

TABLE OF CONTENTS

INTRODUCTION

Why a Book for Parents?

Many books have been written pertaining to the improvement of learning but they have almost always been aimed at the educational establishment; mostly teachers and school administrators. I have concluded that the educational establishment is unable to reform schooling by itself. Many educational conferences have been held during which individual educators have heard research findings that have indicated the need for substantial change in our schools and they resolved to implement the needed changes when they returned to their work place. However, the forces resisting change have been so great that little real reform ever materialized.

Probably no other human enterprise, with the possible exception of medicine, has been researched more thoroughly than schooling. Ironically, no human enterprise has resisted change based upon research findings more than schools. Part of this resistance to change can be attributed to inertia—the human rationale for maintaining the status quo. "We've always done it this way" is a common reaction to any questioning about current practice.

Parents and other concerned citizens have been perplexed at the poor showing our American students display on international comparative tests.

While many educators try to explain away the unflattering comparisons, no one can dispute the fact that about one-fourth of the students in America drop out before finishing the regular high school program. It has also been demonstrated that about one out of five of those students who do receive high school diplomas are functionally illiterate or can barely read at all.

Citizens of the United States must face up to the following:

•The public school system of the United States is failing to prepare students adequately for their future.

•The educational establishment (teachers, school administrators and colleges of education) is unable or unwilling to make the changes necessary to improve schooling without support from the entire community.

•What is needed to make schooling truly effective for all students is a matter of knowledge and not speculation.

•The vast majority of parents are interested in their children's future.

This book is not to be a rehash of the problems of American education but rather, an exposure of

many of the myths that drive current schooling practices, some questions that lay persons, especially
parents, should be asking their local school teachers
and administrators and the answers that will indicate appropriate responses. There are several uses to
which this book is addressed.

Since school reform is so often stalled by pres-
sures from the educational establishment, especially
teacher unions, it is my premise that the last hope
for public school improvement lies with insistent
pressure from the taxpaying public. This book will
give parents the research based rationale to demand
better schools. After all, the schools belong to the
taxpayers , not to educators. Armed with common
sense research-based information parents can become active players in school improvement.

Another purpose of this book is to give parents
a better chance to make wise decisions as to school
choice when the almost inevitable public revolt results in school vouchers or some other alternative to
parents who are tired of being taxed for a social enterprise which is failing. Public schools will no longer
have a monopoly.

This book may also be useful to those parents
who have chosen home schooling for their children.
Solid research will be described which can guide the
planning for and the teaching of children.

Their are several basic assumptions or beliefs that
undergird what follows in this book:

•All students can learn well all that the school teaches.

•School performance is determined, not by aptitude alone, but by both ability—*AND* effort.

•Norm-referenced standardized tests are not useful in measuring school learning.

•Schools are for developing talent; not for selecting talent.
Each of these assumptions will be justified later in this book.

There are thousands of good, conscientious teachers who know that change is needed. This book is prepared to provide parents with a non-confrontational approach to teachers, school administrators and school board members to demonstrate parent support for the needed changes.

COMMON SENSE
AND
SCHOOLS

"U.S. 12th-graders lag world in math, science achievement"

WASHINGTON (AP) -Even America's top high school seniors -those taking the highest math and science courses -performed far worse on an international test than similar students in other countries." (February 24, 1998)

Too many of our youth are reaching adulthood unable to function effectively in their world. As young adults, they remain ignorant of most of the knowledge, skills and habits needed to lead productive and satisfying lives.

International comparative studies of student learning show that this is not becoming less of a problem. United States students continue to rank among the lowest when compared to students of other industrialized nations. Many American educators try to explain away the comparative test results by claiming that other countries test only their best students while the United States sample is more randomly selected.

This explanation, or excuse, is invalid. The sample of students to be tested in every nation included is *randomly* selected. The true sample equivalency is attested to by a separate international selection committee before the testing committee administers the test. In other words, a random sample of thirteen or seventeen year old students is chosen to be tested in each country. Random means that every person in that age bracket within a country has an equal chance of being chosen.

Until recently when we compared the top ten percent of U.S. students with the top ten percent of students from other tested nations, our students compared quite well. More recently even this is no longer true as can be seen by the AP News release above. William H. Schmidt, a Michigan State University professor and coordinator of the most recent math and science international test, reported in 1998 that even our best students fall below the performance of the other tested nations' equivalent students.

So that lay readers can better understand the magnitude of this problem, one question asked students to explain why spike heels might cause more damage to floors than might ordinary heels. Only 42 percent of American students could answer correctly compared to 60 per cent of the international students that energy is concentrated in a smaller area.

For the first century and a half of our history we

needed only about 15 to 20 percent of our populace to be well educated to make our country great. The genius of these leaders developed assembly lines in industry, a powerful military and large religious organizations. This was possible because much of the driving force for these enterprises was hordes of relatively untrained, and often, nonthinking workers or followers.

Technological advances during World War II changed all that. Suddenly schools came under criticism because, in the age of computers and exploding information, we needed most of our citizens educated to the level which only a few had heretofore attained. The pained reaction of most educators was, "Why are we now being criticized for continuing to do what people have previously praised as being a major reason for America's greatness?"

Along with an increasing decline of American education quality, our burgeoning economy is constantly calling for more technically competent workers. As we race toward a global economy where international competition creates pressure on our economy, this educational problem presages an ominous future for our country. Government leaders in the U.S. recognize this need for educational improvement but they continually place their efforts into spending more on school. This approach has proved to be useless for years but a lack of common sense has prevailed.

Further contributing to our schools' problem is

that the citizens of the United States have relegated to the public schools the role of classifier of our ostensibly classless society and the schools have unwittingly accepted this role. How do the schools classify our society? Sometimes in kindergarten, at the latest by grade three, students have been placed into learning groups at schools. While we do not really name them, "Bluebirds, Pigeons and Vultures" everyone knows about the high, average and low ability groups.

Learning expectations are different for each of these groups and teacher expectation is a very powerful force. This classification permanently locks students into high, average and low achievement. There is repeated evidence of very high relationships between the achievement of students at grade 3 and their student rank at grade 11, eight years later. Studies show that the rank order of students within a group of 100 or so students in the same school remains virtually the same for almost 90 percent of the students.

Another finding is that students' academic self concept tends to be relatively positive for *most* students during the first two years of school. But each year thereafter, only the top third or fourth of the students in terms of achievement become more positive about school and about themselves, while the bottom third of the students become more negative about school and themselves. By grade 8, the top students feel very adequate about themselves and desire more education, while the rest of the students have feelings of great inadequacies in school and desire to quit school and school learning at the first opportunity. For the past three decades, 25 to 30 percent of our students drop out before graduation from high school.

Almost all critical decisions in government, industry, schools and society in general are made by that segment of our society which was selected early in their school career to be winners. In an information age, those armed with knowledge and skill in acquiring, organizing and using knowledge have a virtual monopoly upon decision making in our country. The problem this raises is that those in control are quite comfortable with the status quo and those outsiders find themselves increasingly frustrated in attempts to achieve parity. Who among us questions that our country is being divided, ever more sharply, into "have" and "have not" classes of people?

Another very serious problem is the explosion of youth violence. Blame for this is often laid at the feet of drug pushers, broken homes, the economy, loss of values, etc. Another cause which may be the most powerful is the growing disaffection for school among many youth.

The common characteristic of the young participants in violent activity is low self-esteem. There is no more powerful contributor to a positive self concept than the perception that one has some control over one's life and that one is needed and valued by those who are deemed important. Think how helpful young children want to be when given the opportunity to assist mom or dad do some "adult" chore. The problem is that there are fewer adult chores than in the past. Automatic washers and dryers, dish washers, automatic heating systems and power lawn mowers are only a few of the labor saving devices that have made it easier for most Americans. These have also removed many of the chances for children and youth to perform valued services and bask in the resultant adult acclaim. Some of us can recall a time when adolescents were considered an asset to the family because of the important contribution they were making.

Today, there is no socially acceptable role for the adolescent other than succeeding as a student!

By "grading on the curve" more than half the students are labeled as average or below learners. Just being average is not success in anyone's view. Ask adults how many of them are average or below as drivers and you will see how few of them admit to that. But if we graded drivers "on the curve", we know that half or more would be shown to be less than competent drivers.

If the opportunity to demonstrate recognized success is denied to more than half of our youth in school by our traditional ranking system, and it is the only acceptable role for them, what are the natural consequences? Juvenile rebellion, teen promiscuity, violence and drug use are the avenues open to get peer approval and peers are considered significant others to adolescents.

Many of our youth acquire records of misconduct during this quest for some kind of approval from someone that may scar their entire adult careers. Well meaning adults provide adult organized and available opportunities for youth to have what most believe are chances for them to experience success through sports. Common sense should tell us that when the Little League adult supervisors have the games scheduled and the field prepared for play with umpires appointed, the only thing the child can feel will make him valuable is to be sure and make the play or hit the ball. Many kids are unable to experience success even at this. Don't we know from our own youth experience that most of the value of sports came to us in organizing teams , finding and preparing places to play and successfully conducting the games? Most of us recall how important we felt just to have games; few of us can remember who won or who made errors. The fun was in the control we felt to have organized our play. Today the adults in our society have taken away from our youth this aspect of sports programs.

Finally, one must consider the fact that, while many youth are saying they can't find a good job, our classified advertisements are filled with excellent employment opportunities. The problem here is that all good jobs today require knowledge, skill and work habits which the schools have failed to provide to most of their students.

Common sense would dictate that to continue with the present destructive educational processes will only end in a kind of class rebellion and growing inequities in opportunities to lead satisfying and productive lives. The only hope I see to reverse this almost inevitable decline in the quality of life which our youth can expect is for parents to recognize their power to bring about the changes needed in our public schools. *Remember the schools belong to the parents and other lay adults; not to the teachers' unions, administrators or even to the school boards.*

Taxpayers fund schools and should demand those to whom they entrust education to demonstrate how they are doing the job. Typically, educators say that poor educational performance is caused, to a large extent , by the lack of parent cooperation. This defensive position is largely the result of societies' misperception of the roles of teachers and students. Schools are for **student learning.** Using a factory analogy, the product of the school is student learning and not teacher teaching. In fact teaching does not occur unless students learn any more than selling can exist without buying. The school equivalent of the factory worker is the student and the teacher is the manager of these workers. It is up to the manager to lead the workers (students) to produce the product (student learning) efficiently and to be accountable for the amount and quality of output.

By not having clearly understood standards for which to hold the worker (student) accountable no one can know that the manager has not been successful until the product (student learning) is discovered to be unacceptable. It is high time for stockholders (tax payers) to demand that high standards of performance in school be set and that no student be allowed to progress through the system until the student has demonstrated competence in those standards. This would insure that all students earning a high school diploma would have a demonstrated record of mastery of the standards.

Parents and other interested adults should form groups to visit with local school authorities to show their willingness and determination to help the school set standards for the completion of every grade and/or class and support the school when it holds students to these standards. Every teacher (manager) will also be required to report individual student competence in every appropriate standard. Teachers who cannot manage student learning successfully would be identified and replaced. Many will say that this will force teachers to focus only on getting their charges to "pass" the standards—what an improvement that would be! (See Myth No. 3)

At the end of the suggested steps for school improvement are a series of questions that parents, or preferably, groups of parents should ask of their local school teachers and/or administrators. After the questions you will find several traditional educator responses along with a suggested response which you or your spokesperson can use. After each response follows a reference to a more detailed description for why the response is appropriate. It would be well if you and/or a group of interested parents could study this book thoroughly before you approach the school. **Just remember this—The school belongs to you, the taxpayers and not to the teachers, the teachers unions or the administrators.**

EDUCATIONAL MYTHS

All human enterprises are subject to reverence for the status quo. Why, then, is education in the United States so much more resistant to change than most other enterprises?

Schools in America are beset with a plague which has been insidious in protecting current malpractice in education. There are myths about schools and students that many people seem to want to believe. Some of the most powerful and stubborn myths have been periodically exposed for what they are. One can question why the myths persist despite clear evidence that they are untrue.

The satisfaction of parents whose child is in the top or "gifted" class at school is so great that any attempt to radically change the protocols schools now follow will meet strong resistance. Those parents of high ranked students don't seem to realize how poorly their children are really being served. As long as students are ranked against each other, the achievement of the group can drift lower and, though ranking higher is no longer as high as it once was, it gives parents a false sense of pride. Anyone who does not believe this should just talk to some typical high school seniors, who will often brag that they are just "coasting" in their school work and are not really being challenged to learn more. Students included in the recent international tests were asked about how satisfied they were with their schooling and their own achievement. The American students reported much greater satisfaction in their schooling and their own academic success than did the students from the other countries, even though the foreign students scored much higher on the tests.

If high academic standards are set for each grade level and/or class and every student is held to these standards throughout his/her school career, senior level classes will be able to reach much higher levels of learning than is now the case. Parents who are so proud of their child's academic performance should realize that an unacceptable percent of college freshmen are enrolled in one or more remedial classes.

Parents and others who are interested in seeking school reform will have to contend with powerful resistance from another source in addition to the parent protectors of the status quo. Teacher groups, especially those associated with the National Education Association (NEA), do not want any change to occur that will expose individual teacher competence as a manager of student learning. This is a real obstacle.

The many competent teachers in our schools recognize that there are incompetent and/or lazy teachers in their ranks, but orthodoxy in the profession keeps them from endorsing any attempt to install teacher accountability. Excellent teachers should realize that, as a profession, they are being tarred

with the same brush as are the incompetent teachers.

MYTH NO. 1

Myth No. 1: Mental ability limits how much one can learn and it is fixed genetically at birth.

Mental ability as an indicator of learning aptitude has been an unquestioned assumption by educators since, at least, the early 1930's. As France was gearing up for military conflict with Germany before WWI, the government knew that more army officers would be needed.

They also knew that some seemingly objective measurement device should be used to select those French who should be trained to be military leaders. Since the French prided themselves as being a classless democratic society, they were faced with the task of selecting potential leaders that would come from the "upper classes" so as not to upset the social elite and yet would appear to be fair to all. The French psychologist Binet was charged with developing a screening instrument to select the officer trainees.

At the advent of America's entrance to the War, the American government had created a test that would help select soldiers to become officers. A form of this test became the *Otis Quick Scoring Test of Mental Abilities*. The purpose of the test was to discriminate, not to monitor learning or instruction, but schools have used this, or some later derivative, to predict success or failure in school learning.

Dr. S. Alan Cohen, published a booklet in 1987 called *Tests: Marked for Life?* in which he explained his theory about why this type of testing has persisted:

> "How schools and military selection tests became known as intelligence tests is a mystery, but I have a theory. Perhaps the academicians who developed these measures didn't realize their products were made in their own image, so to speak. In other words, university types can be expected to develop scholastic discriminators -tests on which they themselves will perform well. But how did they get other people to accept their criteria as the social standards? How was their way legitimized as the way? 'Divine right' was discredited by the French, American and scientific revolutions. But there was Plato with his myth of the philosopher king, of the 'innate quality of superior intellect.' Perfect for legitimizing the use of instruments as discriminators of human beings. Calling 'it' the skills and knowledge needed to succeed in school would not have been as ego boosting or awe inspiring as calling it intelligence, which sounds like a naturally and genetically endowed gift.
>
> I can't prove my theory, but I do know

that those selection devices have nurtured a belief that has a tenacious hold on the western psyche. No one seems to question that some of us are born with more of that 'thing' than others, and that we need tests to identify it. Tests have resulted in all sorts of inclusions and exclusions. Today, western democracies generate a double elite: those born rich, and those with what most people believe are genetically endowed superior powers. Often people confuse the two; they assume that those born rich also have that natural endowment, or that those assumed to have that endowment are either born rich or destined to become rich. In a society that pays lip service to science and democracy, natural endowment is a convenient substitute for divine right.

The concept of the "normal curve of probability", descending from Mendel's study of genetics, has also distorted the concept of "learning." The definition of the normal curve is that it was a useful method for describing *random occurrences in nature*. The normal curve is useful in predicting natural phenomena based upon the observation of large numbers of subjects. If one knows the height of all the trees in a rural county and plots them graphically, one will likely find a normal curve. That is, a few of the trees would be quite tall, a few quite short and the largest number would be near the average height. This information would be useful in predicting average height of all trees in an adjoining, similar county. However, it would not be useful in predicting the height of a single tree in that second county. One could only say that the probability of the tree being a given height was very low. Also, if the trees in one county had been fertilized (purposely tampered with) the "norm" would no longer apply; the normal curve represents *random* occurrences in nature. Surely education should be more purposeful rather than random.

Schools have used scores from tests designed to produce a normal curve with large numbers of students to predict the academic performance of a single student. This has led teachers to have erroneous preconceived expectations for a student. And this misuse compounds the myth that ability (intelligence) determines learning. Teacher expectations are the most powerful influence in determining a student's aspirations for success.

In 1963 John B. Carroll, in *The Teacher's College Record,* introduced a much needed perspective to the relationship of ability to school learning with a simple formula:

$$\text{Degree of learning} = \frac{\text{Time actually spent}}{\text{Time needed}}$$

Ability is only an indication of rate of learning or speed of perception rather than a measure of how much one can learn. Using innate ability alone to predict how much a student can learn fails to consider the importance of the *effort* a student brings to the learning task.

Benjamin Bloom, in 1968 made clearer the practical implications of Carroll's formula. In a paper entitled *Learning for Mastery* he came up with three propositions:

1. Aptitude can be viewed as an index of learning rate.

2. The degree of school learning for any student is simply a function of the time he or she actually spends in learning relative to the time he or she needs to spend.

3. The time a student spends, as well as needs to spend, in school learning; can be controlled by manipulating certain instructional characteristics alone.

Another way of saying this is that achievement at a high level can be achieved by every student if we are willing to vary the time each student needs. Heretofore, we have had learning time fixed as the same for every student and we have been willing to accept varying achievement.

Schools which have been setting high level learner outcomes at each grade level for *all* students, holding students to these standards and manipulating the time so that each student reaches mastery, have been extraordinarily successful. They have 80 to 90 percent of their students doing as well, academically, as the top 15 to 20 percent of the students in traditional schools. While not a large number of schools nationwide have implemented such a mastery learning program there have been enough, in all geographic and socioeconomic settings, to prove the feasibility of the program for all schools.

Another very important research finding is that the rate of learning does not remain fixed. As students progress through a school where all are expected to master and that is taught, the time required to learn each new task becomes less until, in some schools, all students are learning well at the same quick rate. Student effort can overcome differences in ability if prerequisite skills are not passed over without mastery.

The other part of the myth—that ability or intelligence is fixed at birth and changes little throughout life—has also been proved to be untrue. Studies have been replicated many times to show that measured ability is subject to change. In one such study teachers confused student locker numbers with IQ scores. At the end of the year there was a strong correlation between locker numbers and IQ scores. Students with higher locker numbers were perceived by the teachers to be brighter. They were treated as high ability students and almost all responded by scoring on achievement tests as high ability students. Teacher expectations are much more powerful determinates of how students perform than are ability test scores.

You may wonder how teachers display their expectations to students. Here is one example: Classroom observations show that when a student who the teacher thinks has low ability answers a class question wrongly, the teacher immediately calls on another student. If a student which the teacher believes has high ability gives the same wrong answer to the question the teacher helps them understand the question better and to arrive at the correct response. The teacher will say, "Remember what we were talking about this subject yesterday." or, "Listen to the question again, carefully."

The entire class becomes aware of the teacher's expectations through such responses which are usually not given intentionally by the teachers. Teachers who put great faith in IQ test scores have their expectations distorted by what is reported as ability scores.

MYTH NO. 2

Myth No. 2: Schooling cannot overcome the influence of home and socioeconomic background.

This myth is often expressed as "Schooling doesn't matter." Sociologist James Coleman, in the mid-sixties, published a study in which he claimed that schooling doesn't matter. The socioeconomic stratum into which you are born has more to do with how much you succeed in school and in life than does the quality and quantity of school experience. His studies compared students' socioeconomic backgrounds with their scores on standardized achievement tests. Coleman found there was a high correlation between the income of the family from which the student came and his/her achievement level in school.

Coleman's conclusions were accepted readily in most American education communities. The Coleman Report provided an excuse for not teaching all students to achieve to the same high level. It became a rationale for legitimizing differing expectations for different students. A concluding statement in the Coleman Report sums up the findings thus:

"Taking all these results together, one implication stands out above all: That schools bring little influence to bear on a child's achievement that is independent of his background and social context; and that this very lack of an independent effect means that the inequalities imposed on children by their home, neighborhood and peer environment are carried along to be the inequalities with which they confront adult life at the end of school."

Much of the criticism of the Coleman Report, as well as several other studies done both here and in England, have been directed toward the small sample, the incomplete school reports and some questionable statistical treatment of the data. However, according to Christopher Jencks of Harvard University, "The net effect of the (Coleman) Report's various errors was to *under-estimate* the effect of family background and *overestimate* the importance of school in determining achievement."

The Coleman Report and others commenting on the report provide classic examples of the unquestioning acceptance of certain customs which are in themselves flawed. For the past half-century and more school achievement has been measured by "standardized norm referenced achievement tests." It is long past time to examine the appropriateness of what has been accepted by most educators as the measure of achievement.

The word "standardized" means that uniform procedures and conditions for administering the test have been established. This is a necessary prerequisite to comparing test results among groups or individuals. The real problem comes from the next two words—"norm referenced." This means that the test has been developed in such a way as to allow each person's score on the test to be compared to those of the group of persons on which the test was *"normed."*

The process of developing a norm-referenced test may vary somewhat among testing companies; however, a simplified description of the general steps follows:

1. After deciding what subject matter to test, create test items, ranging from easy to difficult, about the subject. The developers must also keep in mind the age and grade level of students who will take the test.

2. Administer the test items to a representative sample of students to see what percent of the students can correctly answer each item.

3. Items, with performance data, are selected to create a "normal curve of probability." Any items which all students answer or which no students answer, are rejected. A few items which most students answered correctly are selected; a few items which very few students answered correctly are also selected. The rest of the items (about two thirds of the total) are selected from among those items which about half the students answered correctly.

4. These selected items are assembled into a test form which is field tested with representative samples of students. If the test discriminates or ranks stu-

dents from low achievers to high achievers and their performance approximates a "normal" curve of probability, the test is ready to administer.

To accomplish step 1, in this greatly simplified description of norm referenced test development, care must be taken to insure that the test items do *not* measure only what has been taught. If the test measured what had been taught, all students who had been taught well would score high and the normal (bell) curve would be destroyed. Test developers are careful to see that all items relate to the subject tested but they have to include much that is learned "out-of-school" to insure that the normal curve is maintained when the test is given to large groups of students.

If the norm-referenced test measures, to a large degree what students learn outside the classroom, which students are likely to score high? Those students from more affluent homes are likely to have traveled more, have more printed material in the home and have generally more highly educated parents. Is it any wonder that students with higher socioeconomic backgrounds score higher on norm-referenced tests?

Thus we see the myth exposed. Students' scores on norm-referenced tests do reflect their socioeconomic status more than the quality of their schooling because the tests measure so much out-of-school learning. Teacher expectations, which are so powerful in determining school success for the student are tainted by measures which do not reflect what has been taught or learned in school. This vicious cycle feeds on itself and tends to accentuate class divisions in our society.

There is another and even more disastrous result from the improper use of "norm-referenced" tests. Since they are designed to establish that half of the students are above average and half below, they do not provide any clue as to what the "average" is. If education does improve, the tests are re-normed (the term in vogue today is "recentered") up to keep the sacred normal curve intact; the average score is raised. This means that any real and continued improvement is masked. It is surprising that teachers have not noticed that they can never demonstrate real teaching improvement as long as scores are reported on a normal curve of distribution.

Conversely, the decline in education quality that occurred during the 1960's and 1970's was masked because the "norms" were adjusted downward to keep all students at the same relative point on the bell curve. Items that had formerly appeared on fourth grade norm-referenced tests were now showing up on the sixth grade tests to keep half the students above the norm and half below. To see how real this decline was, compare a middle grade history book in use during the 1950's with one used for the same level currently. You will find the reading level of the older book is much higher than that of the books now in use. All during this period teachers could report that their students were performing "at grade level" without parents knowing that the norms for each grade level were lower.

We have all heard educators boast, "we have always had excellent schools; our students have continually scored at the sixtieth percentile on nationally norm-referenced tests." **All this statement can mean is that the school in question has maintained its relative standing on a measure with frequently changing standards.**

How schools can report the actual performance of their students will be discussed in the steps for improvement section.

MYTH NO. 3

Myth No. 3: Teaching for the test is wrong.

Obviously we are not advocating teaching the test, or memorizing the answer to specific questions. This is not what teaching and learning is supposed to be about.

Schooling is probably the only human enterprise where the myth persists that one should not even teach for the test! People who persist in believing this myth usually justify their belief by calling teaching for the test an improper narrowing of the teaching-learning process. " Students should learn much more than I test" is a frequently heard statement from teachers. The accepted theory seems to be that letting students guess what will be on the test is the only way to have students listen to the teacher and to read all assigned material. High test scores are attained by those students who pay close attention and read all assigned material—or by those who, luckily, just learned what was tested.

If one important goal for education is to develop self-directed learners, think how unproductive the usual "guess what you will need to know to pass my test" game really is. A self-directed learner is one who recognizes a problem or a need for information and who can and does proceed, unaided, to solve the problem or get the desired information. To develop skill in becoming a self directed learner requires practice in striving toward a *known* learner goal.

Contrast "Study chapters 8 and 9 for tomorrow" with "Tomorrow you will be expected to list and explain (the test) three important causes for the Civil War. Chapters 8 and 9 will be useful in finding several causes." Which assignment do you think will provide more practice in self-directed learning?

Most who have experienced college "teaching" will recall courses in which no tests were given before the final exam. Even highly motivated and conscientious students will recall their uneasiness in trying to guess what, among all the lectures and reading, they will be expected to answer on the test.

To illustrate how much more motivating learning can be, think of the Scouting Manuals. These publications spell out exactly what skill or knowledge is needed to earn a merit badge. (Incidentally, the same standard of performance is required of every Scout regardless of tested "ability".) Scouts, often with help from parents, can study the manual and practice the skills until they know that they know how to demonstrate their competence before submitting to testing by the Scoutmaster. It has always puzzled me that teachers who have served as Scoutmasters, or had children involved in Scouting, did not see this model as useful in teaching their classes and getting parent help in the teaching/learning process.

Why do teachers persist in playing this guessing game with their students? There are probably some combinations of the following reasons:

1. It is a type of student control through the tyranny of grading. Students will be forced to pay attention, take notes and complete assignments, always searching for clues as to what the teacher thinks important enough to test.

2. If students knew clearly what the expected learner outcomes for a class were, some of them might quickly learn, on their own, to master the desired outcomes and become bored (or a discipline problem) before the course ended.

3. Thinking through why the course is important and what learner outcomes are truly needed by the student and organizing the course so that the learning experiences will lead to those outcomes for all students is hard mental work. It is much easier and much more common for teachers to either teach the textbook or teach what really interests them and then create a test which will array the students along the A,B,C,D and F scale. Since some students will, because of effort and/or luck, score high on the test, the teacher can use this as "proof" that he/she taught the material.

Curriculum and instructional alignment are probably the most productive procedures in improving student learning. When the desired learner outcomes, the instruction and the test are all congruent we say we have curriculum alignment. When the desired learner outcomes are clearly understood, motivated students can often reach them with little help from the teacher. The teacher, in a school where all the students are succeeding, becomes a facilitator of learning rather than the source of information. Teach what you test and test what you teach. This would do much to improve education. This will also do much to focus learning on what is truly important.

Teaching for the test implies that what is tested is truly important. The first question a teacher must answer in planning any unit is: "What do I expect my students to know or be able to do if they master what is important in this unit, be it knowledge, skill, attitude or general competency?" The next question is: "How shall I determine which students have mastered my desired learner outcomes?" and "What will I accept as evidence of mastery by each student?" It is clear that when these questions are answered we have our test. The next step is planning instructional strategies that will be most productive in helping students achieve mastery. **Teach for the test! Students can hit any achievement target that they can see and that stands still for them!**

To further illustrate the sense of the above let us consider this. Suppose a typical college professor was assigned to teach a Driver Education course. The first step the professor would do is to look for an academically challenging textbook. Finding none, the next step would be to write and publish a textbook for Driver Training. The first chapter would probably be devoted to the history of transportation, from the discovery of the wheel to our modern automobile. Next might come a chapter on the mathematics of driving, dealing with such items as the turning radii of the car, the ratio of steering wheel revolutions to the turn angle of the front wheels, the differences in distance traveled between the two rear wheels in different turning situations, etc. Of course there would be an extensive glossary of terms, such as, pitch, camber, toe-in, resonance, etc.

Thank goodness, in most high schools Driver Training is taught by an athletic coach, a person who is accustomed to demonstrating his students' competencies publicly. All he does is have students practice the competencies that will be required to pass the State Driver's License Examination.

Remember a mother does not have to teach her young daughter how wheat is grown and processed to teach her how to make cookies! Teachers need to learn how to focus instruction on what is truly important to enable the student to be successful at the next higher level of learning.

MYTH NO. 4

Myth No.. 4: You can't measure the really important learning in school.

There is a line in the song "Maria" from The Sound of Music which asks the question: "how do you hold a moonbeam in your hands?" The implication is that it is very difficult to quantify or even describe some very important aspects of human character or development. When one asks "What schooling exit goals do we desire for each of our students?" we are really asking "What is the mission, purpose or raison d'etre of our public schools?" While there are some variances among school districts, most schools have mission statements similar to these:

1. All students must have a healthy self-esteem.

2. We expect our students to be able to function at all cognitive levels, in other words to be able to solve problems arising in life using all subject knowledge needed.

3. Students must be able to function at all social levels.

4. Students must be self-directed as learners.

5. Students must develop a concern for others.

These are long term goals; they are the desired results of thirteen years of schooling.

When you plan a long automobile trip to a far distant destination, you next plan intermediate goals; a desired destination for each day's travel, for instance. Similarly, in education we should justify each class we teach in terms of how it will help the student to arrive at mastery of the desired long-term learner goals most efficiently.

There are two aspects of this myth to consider. The term "test" usually calls to mind a paper and pencil exercise. This narrow concept of testing has led many educators to substitute the term "assess" for "test": "I am going to assess student mastery of this learner outcome in this manner." Whether we call it testing or assessment, let us think of some of the ways we can determine student competence:

1. Obviously we can ask students to answer a series of true/false questions. The prevalence of this practice leads to cynicism about reported achievement progress. When one realizes that students have a 50 percent chance of answering each true/false question correctly even if they do not know anything about what is being tested, it is easy to justify cynicism.

2. At the other extreme of a realism scale one

can have a performance test based on reality. The driving portion of the driver's license test approaches reality testing. Obviously, even in a performance test such as driving (or piloting an airplane) one cannot really determine how the applicant would be able to handle a true emergency situation. However, through simulating emergency situations one can come closer to obtaining a true assessment of competency.

3. Writing assessment can best be done by having the student actually write. Even then we cannot be sure that the student will always use his demonstrated competency in writing, but we can know that he/she *could* do so if the student chooses to.

4. Other forms of demonstrated competency are essays and essay questions, oral and written reports, demonstrations, oral and written explanations, self reports, teacher observations and portfolios of the student's work.

All tests are only samples of student behavior. We should always assess student achievement in as near a real life setting as possible within the limits of safety, time available and funding. One of the most common forms of learner outcome assessment when large numbers of students are involved is the multiple choice test. A single multiple choice item can be guessed correctly in 25 percent of the cases. However, when you have four or five good multiple choice test items assessing the same learner outcome -and if you hold that mastery requires getting at least

3 of 4 or 4 of 5 correct you have eliminated the effects of guessing for all practical purposes.

Before reports of student progress gain parent and public credibility, the learning outcome, how mastery of it will be assessed and the standards to be used for reporting mastery must be clearly understood by the lay public, at least the parents. Remember the Scouting Manuals. They clearly explain all of the above and both the student (scout) and his parents know when he/she is competent in the Merit Badge requirements.

Finally, and most importantly, if a test, or some kind of assessment, cannot measure how well a student has mastered important learning goals it means that we cannot really define the goals. Until you can describe how a student who "loves to read" or who "appreciates art" differs from a student who does not, you cannot teach either of the outcomes. When you can describe the difference, you have a basis for assessing whether or not a student can demonstrate mastery—and you can then plan teaching activities that will most likely lead students to the desired outcome.

To illustrate how important learner outcomes can be aligned with instruction and assessment, a study was reported by David Rapaport who is a trainer with Stanford's Accelerated Schools Project. He decided to see if he could teach a total of 65 high school freshmen with ethnically diverse backgrounds to appreciate the humor in a Shakespearean play. He decided that he could only use the frequency and appropriateness of student volunteer laughter as a guide in measuring their appreciation. He video-taped the class upon their first viewing of a scene in "A Comedy of Errors" and carefully recorded the times each student laughed or chuckled. After four class sessions the students then viewed a scene from another Shakespearean comedy, "All's Well that Ends Well", and were video-taped again. The experimenter was able to note that the average student in the post-test scored at or above the point where the highest 15 percent of the students scored on the pre-test. This study is reported in more detail in Outcomes. Winter, 1994. One might argue that recording the students reaction does not really measure appreciation but when parents know what is to be considered mastery of "appreciation" they can judge the teacher's degree of success for themselves.

MYTH NO. 5

Myth No. 5: Multiple-Choice test questions can only measure trivial learning.

One might transform this myth to fact by changing it slightly—most multiple-choice tests only measure trivial learning. This myth has probably arisen and been reinforced by teachers' and students' experiences with norm-referenced multiple-choice test items. Remember that the controlling purpose of norm referenced tests is to rank students from high to low, with one-half of the students scoring above the average and half below. Asking questions about word definitions (vocabulary) and about memorized bits of information (knowledge) are efficient ways to discriminate among learners but they are poor questions to determine mastery of high level learner outcomes.

Contrast the following two test items:

1. About what proportion of the population of the United States is living on farms?
   A. 10 percent
   B. 20 percent
   C. 35 percent
   D. 50 percent

2. *Statement of facts:* The following table represents the relationship between yearly income of certain families and the medical attention they receive.

Family income	Percent of the family members who received no medical attention during the year.
Under $2400	47
$2400 to 5000	40
$5000 to $10,000	33
$10,000 to $20,000	24
over $20,000	14

Conclusion: Members of families with small incomes are healthier than members of families with larger incomes.

Which of the following assumptions would be necessary to justify the conclusion?

A. Wealthy families had more money to spend for medical care.

B. All members of families who needed medical attention received it.

C. Many families with low incomes were not able to pay their medical bills.

D. Members of families with low incomes often did not receive medical attention.

Item 1 only calls for remembering a statistical fact. A student either knows the answer or not. Little thinking is required. Item 2, in contrast, calls for an analysis of the data presented, a knowledge of the processes through which medical services are provided in our Nation and a careful reading of the response choices to select the correct answer.

With care, multiple-choice items which measure higher order thinking skills can be created. Testing higher order skills is efficient because a command of lower order skills simple knowledge about—is subsumed in most higher level items.

Multiple-choice questions can provide useful diagnostic information also:

1.   2.3 + .15=_____

   A. 3.8
   B. .38
   C 1.73
   D. .245
   E. 2.45

(Guskey, p. 40)

A common error students make when adding decimals, especially when they are presented horizontally, is not to align decimal points before adding. If a student chose alternative A or B, the teacher can be fairly certain of the error that was made and can offer specific corrective help.

Constructing criterion or objective referenced multiple-choice test questions that validly and reliably assess higher order outcomes is a difficult task—but a necessary one.

MYTH NO. 6

Myth No.6: Students cannot learn and succeed at school without a cooperative and supportive home.

A few years ago the warden of a Midwest state penitentiary was asked to explain to a legislative oversight committee why there was an increasing amount of violence—stabbings and fatal beatings—among prisoners. His response was that the quality of prisoners he was getting was much worse than in the past. The oversight committee made it clear that the fact that more violent prisoners were being sent to prison was not a valid excuse. The warden was replaced.

This incident may not seem to be related to this myth, but today we are hearing educators using the same excuse—"If you knew the kinds of homes these kids come from you would know why we can't teach them anything." It is true that the children who come from two-parent homes, with only one of the parents working outside the home, is no longer the norm. Schools that haven't changed to accommodate these social shifts do find it almost impossible to serve current students who come to school from a much different environment than in the past.

Up until about thirty or forty years ago, staying in school, at least until high school graduation, was not such a high stake decision. There were still plenty of well paying jobs which did not call for a high level of education. Today we are becoming increasingly aware that both the quality and quantity of education determines the quality of adult life. Yet about the same percent of students (20 to 30 percent) drop out of school before completing high school. In many of our urban centers the percent of students dropping out of school approaches 50 percent.

It is easy to understand how much easier it is to teach students who come from school-supportive homes. We must remember that the parents, both those who are supportive and those who are not, are all products of our schools. Why is it that some homes are so much more supportive than are others?

There are the apparent reasons—single parents, both parents working outside the home, etc.—in fact, many poor parents' concerns for day-to-day survival consumes all their energy and attention. It is also true that most indifferent families are not in such dire straits. The real reason for most lack of school support is due to the teacher's inability or unwillingness to communicate clearly and frequently enough with the home.

Selecting and labeling students in the early grades, through grouping and comparative grading practices, causes many parents to accept relatively low-level academic achievement for their child as inevitable. This removes the high expectations and pressure for the student to do high level work — at least from the home. The parents become satisfied if their child "just passes."

Another, more direct, way in which some teachers discourage positive home support is by contacting the parent only when the child is a discipline problem. This sets the expectation that a call or letter from the school means trouble.

When parents do respond to an invitation from the school for parent/teacher conferences they often leave without clearly understanding what they can do to help. Vague admonitions such as "He needs to get his homework in on time," or "She isn't trying hard enough in school," only causes uneasiness on the part of the parent -and often, inappropriate disciplinary action at home.

Teachers who communicate what the specific learner outcomes they are working on are, what the mastery standards are and then provide frequent feedback on student progress toward these outcomes find parents more responsive and cooperative even when the home situation is not ideal.

Even when cooperation from the home is poor or nonexistent, the school environment can provide frequent success experiences so that the time in school can become the most pleasant and challenging part of the student's day. The most pleasant place most students could be each day is in their school. Frequent success experiences in terms of desired learner outcomes mastered should provide the positive reinforcement needed to keep students learning. When students are constantly compared to other students they lose interest unless they almost always come out on top.

Schools control the conditions necessary for the learner's educational success!

A remarkable movie named *Stand and Deliver* is based on the true story of Jamie Escalante. In this true story a class, not expected to exceed beyond basic arithmetic, is taught through Escalate's rare talent for guiding and inspiring. The students make academic history by record high scores on the State's Advanced Placement Calculus Examination. Rent this movie and see how home environment, while helpful, is not necessary for students to do good work if the teacher sets high goals and helps the students work toward them.

MYTH NO. 7

Myth No. 7: Comparative grading is necessary to motivate students.

When one is asked to justify current grading practices we usually get responses similar to these:

1. We grade to motivate and control students.

2. We grade to label students for certification and selection purposes.

3. We grade to comply with (both imagined and real) regulations pertaining to record keeping and reporting.

4. We grade to uphold our meaning of standards.

The most probable cause is that we grade out of habit, believing that the educational process and system requires the labeling of students.

There are several aspects of present grading practices which work against the setting of educational goals for all students.

1. Because grades are comparisons of the students' relative standing and are not based on objectives mastered, they do not communicate what a student has mastered and/or failed to master. An A grade may indicate the highest

score made on a test but it does not indicate what the student has learned. The whole class may have done very poorly and the highest grade (A) was given to a student who didn't get more than a third of the test questions correct, but since he scored the highest he got an A. In another instance a low grade for certain time period may be a "D" but, because the -whole class scored so high, the student's score may have been above 90 percent correct, but still lower than most other students' scores.

2. Grades, as given now, are permanent. They do not encourage "learning behavior." What encouragement does a student get to continue learning until he/she masters the learning outcome if the grade stays the same? Grades are not related to what a student has mastered or could master.

3. Since teachers' grading standards are based upon so many subjective criteria, grades do not communicate any useful information. Some grades include discipline, attendance, promptness of outside assignments as well as academic achievement as criteria. What does the "grade" mean? Students know that an "A" from one teacher might not rate more than a "B" from another. College and university admissions officers know that the valedictorian from one school district is a much better scholar than the valedictorian from another.

It is almost ridiculous how important we have let our permanent grades become when so much is at stake in our society as to what one's class rank is. Using grades to qualify for certain programs makes grading one of the most important and long lasting effects a teacher has on a student's future.

Letter grades (A,B,C,D,F) or (E,S,M,I,F) have become a shorthand report on student performance. The trouble with letter grades is that no one knows upon what they are based. Do they compare a student's academic achievement with others in the class? Do they reflect deportment or class behavior? How much are they based upon neatness, punctuality, and/or the quality of homework?

Because letter grades convey so little useful information they breed cynicism and lack of genuine motivation. While students begin school wanting to learn, they leave school wanting good grades instead.

Is it possible to have standards and not have conventional grades? Grades and standards are simply different things. To have a real standards system requires clear criteria for student performance. Once you establish learner standards and have a system for demonstrating mastery, all one really needs is a process which records which students have met the standard. They have either mastered the learner outcome or not. These standards should be at the level which we expect our "good" students to reach and our teaching goal should be to help every student reach the same mastery level. International tests show that several other nations are educating all of their students to a high standard; surely American students are just as capable.

Schools which have implemented a standards based reporting system usually report for each student whether or not they have mastered the standard or not. One elementary school which the author is familiar with uses "A" for mastery and "not yet" for non-mastery. The "incomplete" or "not yet" are not permanent; any time a student demonstrates mastery the grade is changed. Think how much more you know about what your student has learned or can do with this type of reporting.

This reporting and recording of student progress by standards met requires that definite observable performance standards are established and can be known to parents, students as well as teachers. On page 153 you will find excerpts of a different type of form for reporting achievement by standards mastered. Most traditional schools do not have these specific standards and this is why states are developing standards for them. Better that each school district establish its own.

MYTH NO. 8

Myth No. 8:
Confusing cause with mere correlation in interpreting educational research.

While this is not as prevailing a myth as some of the others, many educators are unable or unwilling to recognize the difference between correlative and causative research findings. A correlative finding is when a study or observation discovers a correlation between two factors or conditions. For example, most successful professional basketball players wear larger than average shoes. In other words there is a positive relationship between shoe size and success as a professional basketball player. If one does not distinguish correlation from cause and effect, one might suggest that buying all aspiring basketball players larger shoes will significantly improve their game.

This kind of misuse of correlative findings in research has made it possible for both sides of an educational argument to "prove" their points with the same data. A classical example of this misuse is the way the "effective schools studies" data has been used by many educators. During the 1970's, the late Dr. Ron Edmonds and others set out to find the distinguishing characteristics of an "effective" school. Their definition of an effective school was one in which there was no correlation between school achievement and membership in a socioeconomic or ethnic sub-group. In other words, students from poor homes did as well as did the students from more affluent or from the prevailing ethnic majority. They discovered schools which met this criterion but they were few in number. The distinguishing characteristics discovered were:

1. The school climate in these effective schools was positive and focused on student learning.

2. There was strong academic leadership apparent in the effective schools.

3. The purpose of the school, student success, was readily apparent.

4. Teacher expectations for student learning was high.

5. The school measured and reported student success more often than did traditional schools.

The characteristics were labeled clearly by the researchers as "correlates." However, educators began treating them as "causes" for schools to be effective. They began working to install these traits in schools by holding workshops and publishing manuals on how to help a school install these characteristics. No data has been published showing student learning improvements due to the efforts to "install" the correlates in a school. Isn't it time to recognize the correlates as the observable *results* of real school improvements? Schools which have really focused on learning improvement automatically take on the characteristics found in the "effective schools."

Educators are not alone in confusing relationships with actual causes. When it was discovered, during the sixties, that successful workers in industry seemed to have more positive self-images than did less successful workers, many companies sent their workers to workshops to improve their self-concepts. These workers returned to their jobs and no noticeable improvement occurred. It was only during the eighties that industries realized that workers who do good work feel good about themselves, and not the other way around. They then concentrated on helping their workers learn how to do their jobs better and the morale and self-image of the workers showed improvement.

The state of California led the way and the whole nation is following in mounting massive efforts to improve student self- image in the hope that students will then become better learners. This effort is manifest in the many programs that are trying to make students feel ·

better about themselves so that they will eschew drugs. Sooner or later we can expect that they will discover what industry has learned. Students who are successful learners feel good about themselves. Real reform in the way our schools are conducted so that students experience learning success and are not punished when they take a second try to be successful is the most direct way to improve student self-concept and then we will see a real decrease in drug use and other undesirable conduct among our youth.

To further illustrate why a good self-image does not precede good learning, the international test results reported in 1998 showed that while the U.S. students scored at or near the bottom in the world tests of math and science, the U.S. students scored highest at feeling good about themselves and their education.

Good causative research is much more rigorous (and more scarce). It requires controlling all the variables in an experiment, such as setting up identical control groups, and then introducing change in a single variable to see what effect this causes.

One of the most important learner goals every citizen should master is to recognize the difference between correlative and causative research findings.

STEPS TOWARD AN IMPROVED SCHOOL

These are suggestions to follow if you want schools that are truly community schools in all that the term implies. They are actions which involve parents with educators in developing quality learning experiences for all students. It is much easier to point the finger of blame, but unless you can also point the way to improvement you have only started an argument.

One major factor which has led public education to drift so far from its desired function has been the lack of teamwork and a sense of common purpose. Everyone involved - school board members, all administrators, teachers support personnel (secretaries, school bus drivers, custodians and lunch room workers) all need to understand the only purpose for which they exist is to foster optimum student learning. Most often each of these persons has followed a separate agenda. The persons involved in teacher staff development workshops are not the persons who, alone, can make the needed improvements.

The essential criterion needed to implement significant change is the firm commitment from all the persons listed above to improved student learning. Every decision should be studied to see how it will likely impact on student academic achievement. Teamwork can accomplish much more than any one group acting alone.

It is suggested that you recruit some other citizens who are concerned by the declining amount of learning that is now occurring in many of our schools and, if possible some teachers, school administrators and school board members to study the changes suggested in this book. It will take time and effort and you will need a great deal of public understanding to overcome the resistance to change you can expect. You will need to remember that most persons think they had satisfactory school experiences. They will not see the need to change school practices as drastically as this book suggests unless they seriously consider the common sense and the research upon which the suggestions are based.

You will find that most districts have plans for "educational improvement." These may have been developed by a "strategic planning committee." These plans usually focus on cosmetic changes that have been proved to be ineffective. They often include improving physical facilities, smaller class sizes, more "special" classes, improved teacher pay to attract better teachers, etc. They very seldom contain plans for the changes recommended in this book. These committees are usually led by professional consultants who are skilled at leading groups to "feel good" solutions but seldom lead the committee to examining the basic changes that are needed. It is very important that school board members be involved in the change process as much as possible. Perhaps some strong candidates for the school board will emerge as you study and discuss this book.

STEP NO. 1
THE IMPORTANCE OF THE MISSION STATEMENT

To find out whether your local school or school district is succeeding in providing quality student learning one must go beyond just asking parents and patrons what they think about their school. When most U.S. citizens are asked what they think about the American educational system, they will most often reply that it is deplorable. This would be the logical conclusion one with common sense would reach when confronted with the low scores U.S. students achieve on international tests. The same persons who condemn U.S. education generally, almost always say that their local school is the exception.

They believe their local school is doing a good job. Common sense should also tell us that if we think the over-all schools are doing a poor job but that everyone's local school is excellent, we are expecting something that cannot be. United States schools, in general, are made up of many local districts and school buildings. One opinion of our schools must be wrong.

Perhaps this anomaly can be explained because we are all products of a local school and it would be unusual for us to admit that we were poorly educated. There are a few schools, nationwide which are providing quality education for all of their students, but if you seriously consider the aspects of such a school described herein, you will realize that such excellent schools are few and far between.

What should be the mission of our public schools? At a minimum, they should have a commitment, in writing, that every student receiving a high school diploma will be equipped with the skills, knowledge and work habits which prepare them for their future success as students and adults.

Most public school districts do have a mission statement which purports to guide the educational programs in the schools. More often than not these guiding principles include statements similar to this: "We are pledged to develop every student academically to the level of his/her ability."

This kind of statement means that they do not believe that every student can learn well all that the school teaches. With this expectation we will continue to see the decline in the educational development of all students — even those with "high ability" as continually revealed in international comparative tests.

Also, few teachers or building principals justify everything they spend time on during the school day, as being directly related to most schools' mission statements. This is usually because school board members, the overseer of the schools, settle for reports of what processes the schools is following each day and do not demand evidence that students are demonstrating the competencies resulting from these processes. There is a big difference between process and results.

Can you imagine the manager of a baseball team settling for a batter who always holds his bat correctly and assumes the correct stance at the plate but who almost never hits the ball? Of course not; the player is judged (and paid) by how often he hits the ball. A classic example of how we abandon common sense when dealing with education is the millions of dollars we have spent and are spending on the drug prevention program called D.A.R.E. in our schools. Because the program uses police officers in the classroom and students and teachers like it we continue to support the program. What is the purpose of the D.A.R.E. Program? To reduce drug abuse among school age students and to teach the dangers illegal drugs pose.

"Research shows that, no, D.A.R.E.

hasn't been effective in reducing drug use," says William Modzeleski, the top drug official at the National Department of Education. "Its well established that D.A.R.E. doesn't work, says Gilbert Botvin of the Institute for Prevention at Cornell University.

Despite the numerous studies and research showing the failure of the program to produce the results expected, the program remains popular because it makes those in charge feel good that they are doing something to prevent drug use, even if they really aren't.

How does a school district adopt a meaningful mission statement?

Schools belong to and are funded by taxpayers. A group of citizens, hopefully with the blessings of the school board and administration should organize a study committee to develop the mission statement. It will be important to include citizens from all socio-economic and ethnic groups in deriving the mission statement. Teachers and school administrators should be included. Unless the school staff understands the significance of the statement, that all their activities with students should be justified and directed toward meeting the student learning outcomes as stated in the mission for their school, the mission statement will be meaningless. Also, all school staff should recognize that the public will decide how well their school is doing based on evidence that the students are demonstrating that they have met what the mission statement calls for. It will no longer be enough for the school to just annually report input data, ie., class size, per pupil expenditures, staff qualifications, etc.

At the same time the mission statement is being developed, decisions should be made as to how to determine the extent to which the standards are, in fact, being met. A statement that "Graduating students will have a positive self concept" or something similar is included in most school mission statements. How will the owners of the schools know whether this goal is being achieved? This is probably a goal toward which direct teaching is seldom useful, however it is an important outcome. We can judge the progress toward this goal by looking at such data as: Do more students stay in school until they graduate? Is drug use among students reduced? Are there fewer instances of violence in the school? The important thing is that the mission statement goals for students should not just be nice, sentimental statements but should reflect what we really want our schools to accomplish.

Another goal or set of goals in the mission statement will probably deal with academic progress for the students. In the attempt to find criteria for determining success in the goals we should not use statements such as "all students will be reading at or above grade level" at some point in their development. "Grade level" is not really a goal; it is only a position on a norm-referenced test on which the "average" students scored on some test administration. It does not describe a fixed high level of reading comprehension. (See Myth No. 1) A statement such as "all students will have the academic skills and work habits essential to succeed at further schooling and/ or in the work place." This kind of statement can provide a basis for judging how well our school is achieving it. Does a higher percent of our students who choose to go on to higher education succeed more than is currently the case? How many of our graduates have to take remedial courses in college? How do employers rate our graduates in terms of dependability, accuracy and enterprise? These kinds of follow-up studies should be done by every school and the results should help citizens decide whether the school is reaching its mission goals or if there is a need for further change.

Once a mission statement is developed along with descriptions of what it really means in terms of students' demonstrated performances so the public as well as the school can judge how well the school is doing in reaching the agreed upon goals, the statement should receive wide distribution in the community. News media organizations will be helpful in disseminating the statement. Parents and patrons will be helpful in refining the mission statement if given a reasonably convenient way to respond. The mission statement is the declaration of intent for this community's schools.

It may come as a surprise to many that two powerful sources of opposition will come from groups who many think are "friends of education". One of these groups is teacher unions. Teachers individually will be supportive of the reforms needed in our schools, but the leaders of the teachers' unions will recognize it as exposing their members to a degree of accountability now missing in our schools. These leaders have been collecting high dues which pay them good salaries and give them enough discretionary funds to reward some supporting teachers with travel and the illusion that they are in control. Competent teachers recognize how the union shields incompetent or lazy teachers from exposure but they feel afraid to buck the powerful politically skillful union leaders. Parents and patrons should be prepared to deal with this kind of pressure and intimidation.

A second surprising resisting force will be many of the "professors" in teacher preparation institutions. There are so many sources of funding available to them for providing leadership in identifying more and more kinds of "learning disabilities." The very thought of public schools where all of the students are successful learners scares them to death. This opposition is not from everyone who teaches in the colleges or university. There are a few professors who are dedicated to improving schooling and they are producing useful research proving that all students can be successful learners.

The following is offered to illustrate how the absence of agreed upon exit goals can lead instruction far afield. It is not far from the truth!

The Evolution of Math Instruction

This illustrates how far math education has strayed from the purposes for which schools were established:

•*Teaching math in 1950:* A logger sells a truck-load of lumber for $100. His cost of production is four-fifths of the price. What is his profit?

•*Teaching math in 1960:* A logger sells a truck-load of lumber for $100. His cost of production is four-fifths of the price, or $80. What is his profit?

•*Teaching math in 1970:* A logger exchanges a set "L" of lumber for a set "M" of money. The cardinality of set "M" is 100. Each element is worth $1. Make 100 dots representing the elements of the set "M." Represent the set "C", or cost $80, as a subset of "M" and answer the following question: What is the cardinality of the set "P" , or profit?

•*Teaching math in 1980:* A logger sells a truck-load of lumber for $100. His cost of production is $80, and his profit is $20. Underline the number 20.

•*Teaching math in 1990:* By cutting down the beautiful forest, the logger makes $20. What do you think of this way of making a living?

•*Teaching math in 2000 (projected):* By cutting down our beautiful forests a man is making his living. How can we stop this destructive practice?

STEP NO. 2
EXIT STANDARDS FOR GRADE LEVELS AND COURSES

After we have established the exit standards for our school system, along with individual student mastery performance of these standards, we are ready to align all class work with the mission statement. How does this differ from what most schools now do? Today teachers usually choose what they will "cover" in each class by selecting the textbook; the textbook is the curriculum in most classes. The criteria used in this selection process is most usually the following:

- The material should be no more difficult than what the teacher(s) think the average student can master, based on the teacher's past experience. This causes the publishers of textbooks to continually lower the academic content to compete with other publishers who are appealing to the teacher's desire for material that will be easy to "teach".
- The amount of supplementary material such as an explicit teacher's guide with suggested unit tests, workbooks for the

students and other material to ease the teacher's planning for teaching is also very important in selling the textbook.

It is interesting that teachers' unions oppose the state-set learning standards when they so readily accept the standards imposed by textbook authors. Perhaps it is because the state-set standards are usually coupled to some form of school accountability through state tests with published results. States have resorted to setting standards because most local school districts do not have a public set of standards for their students to master.

It requires much less planning time for teachers when they do not have to publicly display the success rates of their students. What they do report is class rankings and honor rolls based on a grade point average that is meaningless in terms of determining how well the school is accomplishing society's purposes.

The most important characteristic of a school which is successfully teaching all its students is that the curriculum and instruction is closely aligned with the exit standards. This alignment is the result of a top down process. This does not mean that the state or school board arbitrarily sets the curriculum. It simply means that we start with the graduation standards and work down through the grades to make sure every thing that is taught is directed toward student preparation for demonstrating competency of these standards. When one is embarking on a long automobile trip, it makes sense to break the trip into what will be traveled each day. If the purpose of the trip is to arrive at the final planned destination on schedule we justify every hour of our travel time as to how it will move us toward getting there.

When we know what competencies the student will have to demonstrate for a high school diploma, we first need to look at what will be taught in the class or grade just preceding the test for graduation. Then we look at the class or course that comes before the final course so that we have passing standards high enough to enable the student, with effort, to succeed with the final course. This process should be followed down through the grades to the beginning. How high should the standard for each class or course be set? The standard should be high enough to insure that the student has demonstrated mastery of the prerequisite skills and/or knowledge needed for success at the next higher level of schooling.

This alignment is very difficult to accomplish and will take considerable time. It will always be open to revision as practice provides data; the important thing to keep in mind is that the **final exit standards should never be lowered.**

After this alignment is accomplished one can then select textbooks that will facilitate the instruction; they should never again be used to dictate the instruction. It may even be that no single textbook will serve as well as parts of several books and other instructional materials such as computers and field research.

To illustrate how this alignment works, here is a description of one school district's plan to provide a closer coupling in their grade level standards with the high school goals. One of the ninth grade standards is for the student to demonstrate how the denotative and connotative meaning of words colors narrative found in newspapers, reports and essays. Beginning in the second grade, students will be taught to differentiate words that are "fact" words from those that are "feeling" words. An exact fact word might be a number such as "seven" or "twelve". A feeling word might be "several" or "few" or "many". In grade five, the students will be taught to identify words that are used in writing to elicit a certain feeling which may be different for others, as opposed to words that have the same meaning to every reader or listener. In grade nine the student will select words and phrases which connote certain feelings among readers or listeners and tell how the author uses them to get a certain reader or audience response. They will be asked to examine research reports to see how words and phrases which are subject to different interpretations are used to influence the reader and to identify words and phrases that are more exact in conveying the same meaning to everyone. They will also be able to use the terms connotative and denotative properly in writing and speaking.

Some may say that this example does not seem to be about a very important issue; however, this district also has an exit standard that every student can actively participate in formal and informal presentations and discussions of issues and ideas and to produce acceptable formal and informal writing.

Another aspect to this process of setting class and/or course exit standards is that teachers will discover how knowledge and competency are actually appropriately integrated across the various domains of learning. Subject matter has heretofore been rather discreetly assigned to specific subject areas. The close relationship between mathematics and science has become more apparent recently. Good writing and communication skills should be a part of the instruction in every subject matter class.

Performance standards for every class and course exit skills that are known , not only to the teacher but to the student and parent at the beginning of instruction, are absolutely necessary if all students are to succeed at the graduation standards. While some will say that it is impossible to set standards in areas such as writing, following is a scoring standard for grade

11 writing that has been in use in Missouri schools for several years. It was established by a large group of communications skills teachers who have demonstrated that when a written example is scored using these standards by many different persons they all reach unanimity as to the value of the writing on a four point scale:

Scoring Guide
Writing Assessment—
Grade 11

4 Points

The paper:

- Has an effective beginning, middle and end.
- Uses paragraphing effectively.
- Contains a strong controlling idea.
- Progresses in a logical order.
- Uses effective cohesive devices (such as transitions, repetition, pronouns, parallel structure) between and within paragraphs.
- Clearly addresses the topic and provides convincing elaboration through specific and relevant details, reasons and examples.

•Uses precise and vivid language.
•Contains sentences that are clear and varied in structure.
•Effectively uses literary and stylistic techniques (such as humor, imagery, point of view, voice).
•Reveals complexity, freshness of thought and individual perspective.
•Clearly demonstrates an awareness of audience and purpose.
•Contains few errors in grammar/usage, punctuation, capitalization and/or spelling.

3 Points
•Has a clear beginning, middle and end.
•Uses paragraphing correctly.
•Contains a controlling idea
•Generally progresses in a logical order.
•Uses cohesive devices between and within paragraphs.
•Addresses the topic using relevant details, reasons and examples.
•Uses precise language.
•Contains sentences that are clear and show some variety in structure,
•Uses literary and stylistic techniques.
•Reveals some complexity, freshness of thought and/or individual
perspective.
•Demonstrates an awareness of audience and purpose.

•May contain errors in grammar/usage, punctuation, capitalization and/or spelling which are not distracting to the reader.

2 Points
•Has a beginning, middle and end.
•Shows evidence of paragraphing.
•May contain a sense of direction, but may lack focus.
•May not progress in a logical order.
•May not use cohesive devices.
•Addresses the topic but relies on generalities (lists) rather than specifics (development).
•Uses general and/or inconsistent language.
•Contains sentences that are generally clear but may lack variety and complexity.
•Attempts to use some literary or stylistic techniques.
•May lack complexity, freshness of thought and/or general perspective.
•Demonstrates some notion of audience and purpose.
•Contains errors in grammar/usage, punctuation, capitalization and/or spelling which tends to distract the reader.

1 Point
•May lack evidence of a beginning, middle and end.
•Contains little or no evidence of paragraphing.

- Is difficult to follow and lacks focus.
- Does not progress in a logical order, and may digress to unrelated topics.
- Lacks cohesion.
- May address the topic but lacks development.
- There is little or no distinction between main and subordinate ideas.
- Uses imprecise and immature language.
- Contains sentences which lack variety and clarity.
- Shows little or no evidence of literary or stylistic techniques.
- Lacks complexibility, freshness of thought and individual perspective.
- Demonstrates little or no awareness of audience or purpose.
- Contains repeated errors in grammar/usage, punctuation, capitalization and/or spelling which are distracting to the reader.

(Missouri Department of Elementary and Secondary Education)

Every graduating student should provide several samples of 4 point writing.

Here are examples of the kind of exit standards being required of the Missouri schools. (This State level mandate would not have been necessary if local school districts had developed there own exit standards for every grade.) You can see how these kinds of exit examination questions will change classroom instruction if students are to be able to answer them correctly:

MATH

Grade four — On Monday Jim sold 6 tickets for the school fund raising event. On Tuesday he sold 12 tickets and on Wednesday he sold 18 tickets. If Jim continues the pattern, how many tickets will he sell on Friday?

Grade Eight — You have been asked to design a rectangular fenced-in playground using the back of the Happy Care Preschool building as one side. The building is 60 feet long. The fence will cost $24 per foot including materials and installation. You have a maximum of $3000 to spend on the fence. The playground must have at least 1500 square feet. Find the dimensions of a playground that will meet these requirements.

Grade Ten — The Silver Peak ski rental shop charges $2 less to rent snowboards than to rent skis and $10 less to rent ski boots than to rent skis. If the total rental price for one set of skis, a snowboard and one pair of ski boots is $54, what is the rental price of the ski boots?

SCIENCE

Grade Three — In what way is it helpful to the polar bear to be white? (Note that these science grade exit questions require a correctly written answer.)

(Grade Seven — A food web illustrates various animals, insects and plants. The owner of a campground where campers have been bothered by stinging and biting insects, suggested that you spray with CT-60, an insecticide that will kill all insects in the area. Other than insects, CT-60 is not poisonous to animals (even those that eat insects). Write a letter to Mr. Crisp explaining how the use of CT-60 could decrease or eliminate the population of rabbits and squirrels in the campground.

Grade Ten — You are driving with your friend, Latonya, on a very cold day. As the windshield begins to fog, Latonya turns on the defroster. In a few minutes the fog disappeared. Use basic principles of physical science to explain what caused the windshield to fog and how turning on the defroster solved the problem.

These questions do not appear on the test but the skill and knowledge needed to answer this type of question should become the focus of teachers who expect their students to do well on such a test.

STEP NO. 3 MATCHING INSTRUCTIONAL STRATEGIES WITH EXIT STANDARDS

There are at least four guiding principals that should be consistently followed in planning instructional strategies if learning success for all students is to be achieved. Number one, all instruction should be directed toward student success in meeting the exit standards. This implies teaching for the test. It also means that teachers of different subjects and, when teachers are teaching all subjects in a self contained classroom, every attempt will be made to emphasize performance in exit standards in every appropriate subject area. Writing a report of a research project in science or in social studies should provide the opportunity to improve writing skills; measurement in connection with a science project should be used to reinforce arithmetic skills, etc. Even music and art provide opportunities to use arithmetic and science.

The second guiding principle is to insure

that needed instruction and review is available on a timely basis throughout the year. If the instruction is carefully planned it will usually occur sequentially; that is, each new unit of instruction will build on the skills and knowledge which the student acquired during the previous unit. This is why it is important to see that every student is ready for each new unit by observing and recording his/her successful performance on the prerequisite skills and/ or knowledge.

Third, teachers should plan to provide a rich diversity of teaching methods to encourage all students to be successful. Education in the one-room rural school of the past provides an excellent example of this. Cooperative learning, students working together to solve problems, was commonplace in those schools. Students can often explain a mathematical solution to another student better than the teacher can. Encouraging this practice occasionally will require teacher and parent understanding of the practice which may be difficult to achieve if they have a strong desire for competition to occur in the classroom. Peer tutoring among students has been criticized occasionally by both the parents of quick learners and those of slower learners. Parents of quick learners say they do not want their child "held back" just to help some slower student. Parents of slower learning students say, "Because my child has more difficulty learning he/she needs a 'qualified' teacher's help, not another student's." It would be well to study some of the research done by Drs. Roger and David Johnson of the University of Minnesota on the practices of cooperative learning.

Dr. Benjamin Bloom, University of Chicago and Dr. Thomas Guskey of the University of Kentucky have been leaders in research in learning for mastery. In the 1960's Dr. Bloom studied what it was that made a student one-on-one tutoring situation so very successful with students with widely varying mental ability. He discovered that it was not the "small" student-teacher ratio in itself that made the difference; it was in the fact that, after the tutor explained each small segment of a solution to a problem, he/she would ask the student to explain the solution back to the tutor. If there was any amount of apparent misunderstanding on the part of the tutee, the tutor would explain the solution again in a different way, so that student understanding of each small step was assured. Because this step is omitted in most classrooms, only a small percentage of the students in the class do learn all that the teacher thinks is being taught. **Remember: if teaching does not result in learning, then teaching has not occurred.**

Guskey's Model
Illustrating Usual Classroom Practice 1.

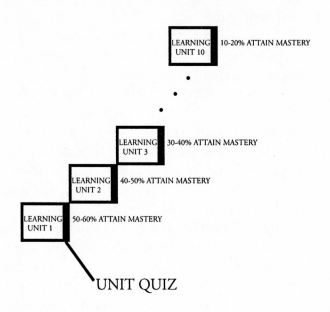

LEARNING UNIT 10 — 10-20% ATTAIN MASTERY

LEARNING UNIT 3 — 30-40% ATTAIN MASTERY

LEARNING UNIT 2 — 40-50% ATTAIN MASTERY

LEARNING UNIT 1 — 50-60% ATTAIN MASTERY

UNIT QUIZ

1. Guskey, Thomas R. Implimenting Mastery Learning, 1997. Belmont, CA.

Guskey's Model
Illustrating Mastery Learning

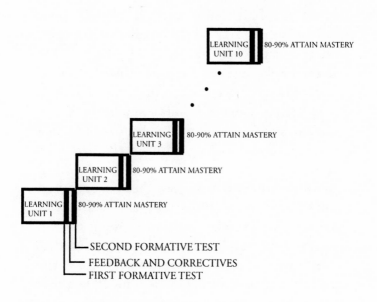

1. Guskey, Thomas R. Implimenting Mastery Learning, 1997. Belmont, CA.

It can be seen from Figure 1 that even if the average teacher gets 60% or more of their students to master the first of a series of sequentially more difficult concepts, the second unit will have fewer successful learners because 40% of the students do not understand the pre-requisite material for succeeding at the second level, etc. This results, after a series of units, where only about 10-20% will have learned what the teacher "taught." The bell shaped curve or the normal curve of distribution describes random occurrences in nature. Common sense tells us that schooling should be a purposeful activity rather than a chance occurrence.

How does teaching for mastery provide for at least 90% of the students performing as well as those students who have been taught by a competent private tutor? The usual instruction in our schools today is paced at about the rate at which the teacher thinks the average student can learn. As you can see from Figure 1 this results in a class average that is much less than the teacher "covers" in his/her teaching. By following a practice illustrated by Guskey in Figure 2 we provide for varying the time spent in instruction to reach the desired mastery by all students. This may seem to slow the rate of instruction to the point that quick learning students will be held up in their learning. What actually occurs is that when every student has the pre-requisite skill and/or knowledge to successfully master what is being taught, not nearly as much time needs to be spent by the teacher trying to remediate those students who do not understand the current instruction. The other advantage to teaching for mastery is that, as students are experiencing continued success, they are motivated to exert more effort to keep on succeeding. Learning requires both ability and effort and effort can and does overcome differences in ability to the degree that all students can learn well. Remember that some shorter basketball players can successfully compete with taller players by exerting more effort.

Learning for mastery involves teaching the unit the best way the teacher can organize the instruction. Then a quiz is given to provide feedback to the teacher so that those students who mastered the material can be identified. Those students who do not demonstrate mastery of the unit on this first quiz are then given corrective activities that are different from the first teaching strategy used. Those students are then given another quiz and then the teacher moves on to the next unit of instruction. One might ask, what happens to the student who also falls short on the second quiz? They are moved on to the next unit. All material is not clearly sequential and during the next unit or two the student who did not demonstrate mastery on either the first or second unit quiz will be able to demonstrate that he/she now does understand what he/she had formerly missed. During the one or two periods that the teacher is providing the needed corrective instruction, those students who demonstrated mastery on the first quiz are given enrichment material that is interesting to the student and which challenges her/him. This actually results in increased learning for all the students and almost guarantees that all students will demonstrate mastery of the exit standards for the grade or class. It is recommended that one read one of Dr. Thomas Guskey's books describing the process of teaching for mastery in greater detail.

Even though teaching for mastery has proved over and over again that 90% of the students can demonstrate on a performance test that they can do as well as the top 10-15% of the students are now doing, and common sense tells us it is a better way to teach, some teachers will have objections to the practice. Some will say that we should record the first quiz score in the permanent record book to show which students are doing better. That first test in each unit is to provide the teacher with an indication of how effective the teaching has been and to help select students who need correctives and which need enrichment. The first quiz is also an indication to the student of what the teacher thinks is very important and it also shows her/him which of these important learnings he/she has mastered already and which needs more work.

Teaching for mastery is hard work and requires the teacher to use great care in preparing the test so that it really measures a step toward the exit goals for that class or grade. It is more a measure of teacher effectiveness than of student merit. It also requires careful planning to provide enrichment activities for the students who do not need correctives. It should be something that students want to do and it should challenge them enough to let them feel that they are not wasting time. If teachers of the same grade levels or subject matter work together and share ideas it can become a team effort to see how much they can raise student learning.

Some may have reservations that following such a precise series of mastery learning steps may make transferring from school to school more difficult for a student. The author was high school principal in an American Defense Department School in France for a year and was Assistant Superintendent in the European Area with headquarters in Germany later. There were 140,000 students and 7,000 plus teachers in these schools from Oslo, Norway in the North to Peshewar, Pakistan in the South. Students attending these schools had been transferred from state to state in the U.S. And from country to country abroad and they had little trouble adjusting to their new school. Schools which have set their academic standards for each grade level carefully will find their standards are very similar to those of other districts.

The fourth important aspect of Step 3 is that teaching for mastery provides more than one uniform, routine chance to be successful even after regular reporting periods. There is no incentive for a student to work to improve his/her record if they have already been marked permanently as being slower than some other students.

In mastery learning situations the number of students needing corrective work becomes fewer and fewer. This is because students who are naturally slower in comprehension have learned that if they put forth more effort they can keep up with the faster learners. One can only imagine the despair some students now feel when in classes where, because they didn't have a chance to learn well the last unit, they are faced with class discussion, reading or teacher lectures that they cannot follow. Again common sense tells us that it is no wonder so many students drop out or want to quit school.

One of the objections that some teachers have, especially in the middle and upper grades, is that many students just do not try and mastery learning will not work with them. Their experience with these older students only illustrates the problems with schooling today. Students are permitted to get so far behind in their learning and have been passed on. These students have experienced failure so much by not being held to high learning standards that they do not believe they can be successful students. Schools need to hold students for high performance at every grade level so they know that, with effort, they can be successful.

Fine arts performing groups such as the band or orchestra are demonstrations of learning for mastery. Both the teacher and the students in those organizations know what the performance goals are; they can hear excellent recordings of how the music they are assigned should sound and they can work together to "pass the test". Some students have to practice more than others but the goal is to get every student to play his/her assigned part in concert with the others. Think how much most students enjoy these classes and how few want to quit the organization. Also, by publicly demonstrating the music teachers effect on students, parents can hold the teacher accountable for the desired results. Competent teachers would be proud to have the same opportunity to demonstrate their students' competency on agreed upon standards that are objectively judged.

No school, classroom or teacher can learn for the student. Learning is a personal accomplishment. Time allowed for learning can be increased if student perseverance is improved. In education we have called this student willingness to persist in learning motivation. The aspect of telling the student exactly what the mastery standards are is such a powerful motivator that students who have learned to believe they can learn will often achieve the desired competency on their own with little or no help from the teacher.

In a traditional classroom there is little a student can do to change his/her perception as a successful learner. The student is continually compared to other students and this relative standing will change little over time. When each student is striving for the same known high level standard of performance, and success is assured even if the student takes a little longer time to demonstrate competence, he/she will persist in seeking mastery. Learning success should be controlled by the student's effort and not by the teacher's ranking based on the time it takes for mastery.

A success experience in a domain of learning does have a positive motivating effect on the student to attack positively the next learning experience in the same subject. This is especially true if the student attributes his/her success to conditions over which he/she has control.

Attribution theory states that it is not an experience (success or failure) that tells how a student's motivation will be affected. It is essentially *why* the student believes the experience occurred. Knowing why the experience occurred or knowing the major reason for the experience occurring helps to understand the motivational effect for the future.

An example of a success experience for a student might be receiving a perfect score on a test. Here are some of the reasons this might have occurred:

1. The student copied answers from another very competent student.

2. The student found a copy of the teacher's test key and copied the answers from that.

3. The student luckily only studied part of the textbook but it was the part over which the test was constructed.

4. The student listened well and took careful notes during the class, studied each assignment conscientiously and reviewed all of the material before the test.

The same experience occurred in each instance - the student received an A, but think what a motivational difference the experience can provide depending on which circumstance the student attributes the A grade to.

According to most attribution theorists, the best reason to believe you succeed is ability. You did well or you won the competition because you have the talent and ability to do well. This will generate some degree of pride because it is your ability. The locus of control is within. In addition, ability is stable; if you swam fast today you can still swim fast tomorrow. This engenders confidence. Pride and confidence are powerful motivators for persisting in an activity.

What if you do not win the race? To what do you attribute your failure experience? Ability, or lack of it, is probably the worst reason to believe you have failed. You have to look at yourself and say "I don't have the ability." You can't blame anyone else so there will be some degree of shame. And, because ability (or lack of it) is stable you realize that you cannot develop it overnight. This is likely to cause some depression. Think what schools do when they label some child learning "disabled."

There is another attribute which people believe contributes to both success and failure. That attribute is effort - or lack of it. You succeed because you trained faithfully. You gave the activity all you had and you never gave up. This was your effort. Again the locus of control was within and results in pride. What if you attribute your failure to win to lack of effort? You didn't train properly. You didn't give it all you had. This will result in some degree of guilt, but because effort is within your control you can have some hope that if you try harder you can do better.

Learning to master set standards helps all students realize that competence as a learner is a matter of effort as well as ability. Slow learners in such a classroom soon learn that they will achieve success eventually and that by exerting more effort they can learn how to learn more quickly. Experience demonstrates that in a class where standards are set the same for all students, students learn to compensate ability with effort and more students perform like the fast learners now do.

STEP NO. 4
DEVELOPING A SYSTEM
OF ASSESSMENT

A record keeping system should be developed that is manageable for the teacher and which communicates to the student and parent precisely which of the course or class performance standards the student has mastered. This can be done if a clear set of performance standards is established for all exit standards. Whenever a student demonstrates mastery of an expected learning outcome it will only take a check-mark or the recording of the date for that standard for each student. In short, a good student record system will document what a student can do successfully whenever they are able to do it. Computers now make possible the record keeping for each student. A computer record keeping system will make it possible to pull up any student's record for parent conferences so that a constructive plan to strengthen the student's performance can enlist the parent in this effort.

When the student realizes that it is his/her responsibility to meet the competency standards for each grade level or class before moving to a higher level or before receiving credit for the class in high school, she/he will begin to accept the responsibility for learning and exert the effort needed to "keep up". Students need to know how high the bar is set in every class to know how high they are going to have to jump to clear the bar. This makes so much more sense than just working to receive a grade based on relative standing in the class, with no regard to what a fixed standard is.

Frequent diagnostic checks of student understanding and/or competence is necessary if the student is not to fall hopelessly behind. The motivating power of seeing progress frequently causes students to see learning as enjoyable, even if difficult. Teachers who object to taking time from teaching to do frequent testing should look at the percentage of time a physician spends in testing compared to the time the doctor spends in providing treatment. The medical doctor is interested in treating only that which needs treatment. Even the more able students do not enjoy school when much time is spent going over material that they have already mastered.

The records should enable students to demonstrate and receive full, credit for improved learning on a timely basis anytime prior to graduation. Only if this is possible and understood by the students can we expect them to continue to strive for mastery. The record system should indicate just which of the exit standards the student has mastered rather than an invidious comparison with other students.

Page 147 illustrates one method of reporting for a school or classroom, assuming the students are assigned to teachers randomly and not grouped by "ability."

STEP NO. 5

ONGOING SYSTEM
OF
PROGRAM
DEVELOPMENT

As the first four steps are being developed we should begin to develop an ongoing system of program development. Teachers, administrators and most adults will be brought to face the fact that many current school practices are based on customs and myths which have no support in reality. Overcoming the hegemony of education's past will not be easy. At one of the early meetings of parents with school staff members it is recommended that a rule be established: No argument should be made in support of or against the changes recommended in this book without supporting research to back up the argument. We should always be striving to base any changes suggested on the latest knowledge and credible research findings. It might be wise to look at the differences between controlled experimentation and just random correlative research results. (See Myth No. 8)

Staff development should be planned to

reach an exit goal the same way that teachers should plan what happens in the classroom. The standard that should guide every staff development activity should be: **All staff members should be using the best available knowledge to develop course and unit outcomes for all students and other key indicators of school effectiveness which are used and updated regularly to improve the conditions and practices that affect student and staff success.**

Changing the mind set of teachers who have used textbooks as the major source of the curriculum will be difficult. When doing workshops for teachers the author has heard many of them state something like this: "I don't know when we are going to find time to teach students to perform well on these standards when we have so much else to teach."

When asked to describe what the "else" is, the teachers would usually say that they felt compelled to continue "covering" all the material which they had done before or that was in the textbook before they could teach for the newly developed standards. They could not see that what we were proposing was to take the place of what they had been teaching. Teaching for exit standards does not mean that all old skills and knowledge should be eliminated. It simply means that we should make sure that everything which is important for the student to master at that time to be ready for her/his next higher level of learning is really *taught* to every student.

Teachers will need help in developing assessment strategies that provide clear and understandable evidence as to which students have demonstrated mastery of an outcome and which have not. (See Myth No. 4)

Teachers are accustomed to objectives that state something like, "Students will understand the U.S. Constitution." This nebulous statement is virtually meaningless. What does 'understand' really mean? How will we recognize which students 'understand?' Almost anything the teacher does in the classroom can be justified as teaching for this goal as long as it has something to do with the U.S. Constitution; this could include having the students memorize the preamble to the Constitution or the Bill of Rights. These activities probably do not lead to understanding but they may make the teacher feel like they do.

A much more meaningful standard might be: "Each student will demonstrate an understanding of how the U.S. Constitution guides decision making in the U.S. by taking a recent Supreme Court decision and describing which article/s or which one of the Bill of Rights were used to justify the decision and what likely effect this decision will have on our society."

Think how this type of unit or exit standard would focus the instruction. It also conveys to the student what the importance of the Constitution is and how they should examine a decision. It also communicates to the public what we mean when we report that X number of students "understand the U.S. Constitution."

We can see how this kind of careful construction of learning standards takes time but can be worth the effort in focusing student efforts toward the standard. It also makes it possible for the student, and a parent who wants to be helpful, to know when the student knows enough about the Constitution and is ready for the assessment process. Think how much more control you would have felt in school if all your learning objectives had been so constructed.

Another prejudice that has developed over the years in education is the belief that if a student is given a grade it can never be changed. The permanence of a poor mark has kept many students from seeking to improve their performance. The author has seen the remarkable improvement in student writing when they are shown how to better their performance and receive credit for the improvement. When given a paper to write as an assignment, I would carefully read each paper and record, on the paper, what needed to be done to improve the paper. Then I would assign a letter or number grade.

If the paper was quite good and the student received a high mark, he/she was through with the assignment. If the student received a low mark, he/she could use the suggestions recorded on the original paper, rewrite the paper and resubmit for evaluation. If the rewritten paper now received a higher mark, this higher mark was recorded for the record. If the student did not choose to seek a higher mark by rewriting the paper, the original low mark was recorded for the student.

I was criticized by colleagues for this practice for two reasons: The student had little incentive to do a good job on the first attempt when he/she would receive suggestions for improvement and could do the paper over. The students soon learned that if they did not want to do the paper over they had better get it "right" the first time and student writing improved. The other criticism was that it was unfair to the student who did a good job the first time for the other students to be able to get an equally good mark on a paper which was redone. My answer to this was that I was in the business of teaching students to write better papers and not in the business of ranking students.

Changing teacher attitudes from that of *selecting* talent to that of *developing* talent may take time and effort but the change can be facilitated if parents are supportive of the process. This requires the change in the attitudes of parents also. Those parents who now don't care what the students have learned just so long as their child gets higher grades than most students may find the change especially difficult.

STEP NO. 6

SECURING AND RETAINING QUALITY TEACHERS

Parents and a cooperative board of education can plan to identify and reward competent teachers to a greater extent than is now the common practice. One of the most important steps to take in this regard is to secure from the school and district how much the total expenditure for the school and district is per child enrolled. Next we need to see what percent of this total per pupil expenditure is actually used for classroom instruction. Fixed expenditures such as debt service, insurance, building maintenance, school bus transportation, janitorial services and school lunch costs should be subtracted from the totals. Next we should separate out administrative costs which will include all building and district professional and support staff and make a note of that. All this data should be publicly reported, at least annually, to the entire community. This will focus attention to what is actually available for managing student learning in the classroom. (In school districts where this is the practice, it is remarkable how many administrators and supervisors find they can operate quite well with fewer secretaries.)

When beginning teachers are employed we should assign them to small classes (15 or 20) where they are paid what the actual instructional costs are for this number of students. They should each also be assigned to a mentoring teacher who will be paid extra for helping the new teacher to be successful. If the students of this first year teacher demonstrate that they each have met the exit standards (see Step No. 2) at the end of the year the teacher should be assigned more students for the coming year, with the commensurate pay increase. This contrasts with common practice in many schools today where beginning teachers are assigned the least desirable students and classes. Common sense should tell us that this is not the thing to do.

As the entering teacher demonstrates her/his competence through demonstrations of student mastery of the exit standard for the class, they should be given more students with the instructional funds generated by the larger class. This could lead a master teacher to be assigned responsibility for larger numbers of students with funds to employ aides if needed so long as all of his/her students are meeting the mastery standards. Teaching could become a real profession under such circumstances. This kind of system would also allow for those competent teachers who did not want to teach full time to teach part time, maybe only a half day or a few classes and still be paid what the instructional time and numbers of students generate.

The teacher compensation plan listed above would threaten the single salary concept that has become so entrenched in our schools. It would even challenge state set minimum salaries for beginning teachers. Change is not easy, but the present system is not working.

It defies common sense to believe that teachers who are not effectively teaching students should be paid as much as those who are. With a way to demonstrate objectively how competent teachers really are we can justify these needed changes. If a district has undertaken steps 1 through 5 they will be ready to discuss alternate ways to compensate teachers. Also the annual report of the school budget recommended above will cause a close examination of how much administrative overhead actually exists. Comparisons among schools and districts in this regard have almost always resulted in a lower percentage of the budget being spent on administration. Subject area specialists will now be able to demonstrate how their services have improved student performance or it will show that they have not.

Perhaps this step will meet greater resistance from teacher union organizers than any of the others, because it may point out that the individual teacher is more responsible for how well they are compensated than is the union, and the dues aren't so high. With excellent teachers in such short supply, they do not need union protection. Unions were created when the worker had no leverage in dealing with management; they exist today, among teachers, primarily to shield the incompetent teacher from public scrutiny. Our schools should be the result of the cooperation of the lay public, the school board, parents, teachers and administrators. They are all members of the same team working toward a common goal—student learning. To the extent this is not true in your community, change is needed.

Parents, or groups of parents who have studied this book, should now be prepared to ask for an appointment with the school superintendent or the local school principal to ask and discuss the following questions. This meeting can serve to let the school personnel know that you are willing to work with them in school improvement and that you are armed with knowledge to contribute to the discussions.

Anyone familiar with professional educators will know teachers' unions have staunchly resisted any attempts to operate schools in a framework where teachers have real accountability for student learning. The leadership and many members of the American Federation of Teachers (AFT) have endorsed most of the ideas presented in this book, but the National Teachers Association (NEA) have, since the late 1960's, resisted any change which might make teachers accountable. Parents should be prepared to encounter fierce resistance to many of the proposed changes found in this book; but just remember **these are your children and this is your school and you are paying the costs—** it just makes sense that you should prevail in your quest for improved school learning.

QUESTIONS TO ASK OF YOUR SCHOOL

Question No. 1

Do you believe that all but about three or four percent of the most severely mentally handicapped students can learn all that the school teaches?

Answers to be expected from teachers or administrators in most schools:

•Of course we believe that all students should succeed to the level of their ability.

Your response: When you say "to the level of their ability" you are implying to us that you have different expectations for your students and they will not all be expected to learn all that the school teaches.

•They can learn it, but at different levels because their abilities differ so much.

Your response: Research indicates that teaching strategies being used in some excellent schools are resulting in eighty-five to ninety percent of their students achieving at the level at which the upper fifteen percent of the students now perform in most schools on standardized norm-referenced tests.

•If you could see the homes that some of our children come from you would understand why they can not learn very well.

Your response: If schools -do not now control the conditions for success what do we need to do to change them so that they can? Dr. John B.Carroll introduced a perspective back in 1963 that explained that the degree of learning which any student experiences is simply due to the time he/she *actually* spends in learning relative to the time he/she *needs to spend.* In other words, aptitude for learning is only a measure of an individual's learning rate. Aptitude is not a limiting factor in how much one can learn if the proper amount of time is provided. *Schools do control, the amount of time spent on learning.* (See Myth No. 1 and Myth No.6)

•If we provide the amount of time needed by slower students we will hold back the learning progress of the brighter students.

Your response: Brighter students (faster learners) are handicapped and held back now in schools where teachers "teach to the average." So much time is devoted to remedial instruction for those students who have fallen behind that the whole class moves more slowly. Furthermore, those students who start out as slower learners can actually begin to function on a par with faster learners by exerting more effort. This will only occur if the student has perceived him/her self as a successful learner because the teacher made sure that he/she understood before moving on. Schools where this concept guides instruction actually have *all* students achieving at a higher level than the "bright" students now attain. When every student has mastered the prerequisite skill or knowledge needed to study more advanced material the entire class will move along faster because so much teacher-time will not have to be spent on remedial instruction.

•Intelligence (IQ) tests that show that some of our students should not be expected to achieve at a high level.

Your response: IQ tests have been shown to be a measure of the student's speed of perception and socioeconomic background. They are not an appropriate test to set teacher expectations which are the most important determiners of a student's scholastic success. IQ tests do not measure how much a student can learn; only how fast one learns. The amount of time a student spends can be controlled by the school by manipulating instructional characteristics alone.

Question No. 2

Will you describe the grading system which is used in your school?

Answer to be expected from teachers or administrators in most schools:

• We use the letter grades of A,B,C,D and F for students in grades one through twelve. In kindergarten we use + or - to indicate how the student is doing.

Your response: We believe that parents should be given frequent reports on the specific learner goals their child has demonstrated mastery of and those on which he/she needs more work so we can help them at home whenever possible. (See Myth No. 7)

Question No. 3

Can you explain what the letter grades used on the report cards mean to a parent?

Answer to be expected from teachers or administrators in most schools:

• Of course an A grade means that the student is achieving at a level which is among the highest in the class. Other letter grades represent achievement that is at a lower level.

Your response: This implies that the grade received is relative to the other students in the class. We believe that parents would much rather know exactly which specific skills or knowledge for which their child has demonstrated mastery. How the student compares to other students does not really tell us whether the class as a whole learned well or not. It also does not tell us what we can expect our child to do to demonstrate his/her mastery. (See Myth No. 7)

Question No. 4

Will you share with us the expected skills and/or knowledge which every high school student is expected to demonstrate mastery of before he/she receives a high school diploma?

Answers to be expected from teachers or administrators in most schools:
•Students must receive a passing grade, at least a D, in every class or grade to be passed on to a higher grade. A student must "pass" the required number of courses in high school to receive a high school diploma.

Your response: This still does not give us any specific learner outcomes which we can expect our students to have mastered. It will be impossible for us (or a prospective employer) to check whether our child can perform specific tasks or to solve specific problems unless we can know, not only what the learning goals are, but how competency has been measured.

Question No.5

Can you provide us with a list of performance standards every student must meet to be promoted from grade to grade or to receive credit for on the student's H.S. Transcript?

Answers to be expected from teachers or administrators in most schools:

•We have district curriculum guides which list all topics that are to be taught in each grade or class. We can show you a copy of these.

Your response: These guides only list what will be "taught" in each class and/or grade; they do not tell us what will be "learned" by every student. They also do not tell us how mastery of each learning standard will be determined. How will we, as parents, know whether the school is delivering what it purports to deliver?

•Because students vary so much in ability it would be difficult to say what every single student will have mastered.

Your response: With this explanation there is no way to see how well our school is doing its job. It also makes it difficult for employers to know what skill or knowledge a job applicant has, even if he/she has a high school diploma. As parents, it will be very difficult for us to help our children reach these performance standards if we do not know what they are.

•We do expect every student to achieve a passing score on tests which are given, both teacher made and standardized norm-referenced tests.

Your response: If students do not know what they will be asked to do on tests how can they prepare to do well? The result is a guessing game between the teachers and the students.

Question No. 6

Is the grade a student receives on a course or class final test permanent? Does the student have a chance to raise the grade if the student demonstrates that he/she can now answer the questions missed on the test?

Answer to be expected from teachers or administrators in most schools:

•We are required to keep a permanent record for each child. A part of that record is their grades on important tests. If the student later learns to perform at a higher level it will be reflected in future scores.

Your response: If the student is returned a written assignment which has a number of errors, and he/she knows that the grade received for that paper is recorded permanently, what incentive is there for his/her to correct the errors marked on the paper? If one is trying to teach a student to write better we think they should be allowed (encouraged) to use the teacher's marked errors to rewrite the paper in a better form and then be recognized for this improvement. We think the school should help *develop talent* and not just to *rank students* (See Myths Nos. 3 and 7).

CHANGES NEEDED IN TEACHER EDUCATION

Institutions of higher education which train teachers must be changed drastically if they are to continue to be a major source of teachers. Today, with the blessings of the state departments of education, schools of education at the college or university level are about the only source of teachers. What are they doing wrong?

One of the problems of teacher education programs in almost every college or university is the lack of a broad general liberal arts background for every prospective teacher. Students begin specializing during their first year or two in most schools. This has been made necessary because of the proliferation of courses required for special certification. A student planning to become a high school science teacher will very soon be advised to begin specializing in a discreet science such as physics, biology, chemistry, geology, etc. This results in teachers prepared to teach only one of these subject areas. A further problem with the present system is that prospective teachers are marched through the same courses as are those who aspire to be a nuclear physicist. The needs of teachers of K-

12 science are quite different from those of the Ph.D candidate in biology, physics, chemistry, geology, etc. College professors, especially at the graduate level, are engaged in preparing specialists to learn more and more about less and less.

Prospective teachers are assigned to a faculty advisor in the field of study in which they plan to major. These professors often urge their advisees to take all the courses in the field which most interests the advisor. Students who plan to teach math, science, social studies or in the fine arts seldom get the well rounded background needed to succeed in teaching elementary or secondary students. A check back at the records will reveal that, until about forty years ago, high school graduates scored much higher on more difficult tests over a wider range of subjects than current graduates. While schools in the past may not have offered the wide range of classes that are now offered they did teach all the students needed to know to succeed in college or in the work world and without so many remedial courses being needed.

Colleges and universities which are preparing teachers need to see that the students can teach good writing and speaking skills and are well grounded in the history and culture of their country as well as be specially trained in a narrow teaching field. It used to be that a high school had a music teacher who taught both the instrumental and choral performing groups. Today we find some high schools with brass instrument or single reed specialists. Perhaps we should see if the public school is the place to develop solo artists or if that purpose should be better served by private instruction when warranted. It is alarming to note that many of today's high school teachers are so ignorant of great works of literature, of the persons who contributed so much to our country through their writing, and of the important events that have shaped our Nation.

One other problem encountered in teacher preparation at many of our large colleges and universities is the lack of attention paid to the freshman and sophomore classes which are supposed to provide a liberal arts background. Department chairmen and tenured professors are so interested in securing funds to do research and writing that they often assign graduate students to teach these general education classes. These teaching assistants (TAs) are interested primarily in completing their own graduate program and are not as well prepared to teach as they should be. With this most recent model of teaching before them, it is no wonder that graduating teachers do not use the best practices in their own work.

Very few colleges or universities are preparing teachers to develop learning standards which can be observed and objectively assessed. They are not preparing teachers to utilize criterion-referenced or performance based assessments to check on their own teacher effectiveness and to provide instruction appropriate to the student's level of achievement. Teachers are still being taught research methods and statistical treatment of the obtained data that reflect the "normal curve" or that are appropriate when measuring random occurrences in nature. This treatment of statistics may be appropriate for scientists, economists and meteorologists but is not all that a teacher needs to know about assessing the degree to which each student meets a learning standard. Perhaps we need some specialized teacher training institutes which recognize the problems with most programs today. This certainly does not mean that we need to add more "education" courses.

Remember how successfully a mother with little formal education can teach her child to make cookies? This is because the mother knows what essential skill and knowledge is necessary to make cookies and she concentrates on these in her teaching. Teacher training candidates should be able to experience college instruction that is based on what a teacher needs to be able to do on the job; this does not require a lot of specialized courses but, rather needs modeling by a competent teacher in college.

A few teacher training programs use an exchange system with one or more good public schools. A college professor in the school of education and a successful classroom teacher occasionally switch roles for a period of time. This keeps the professor abreast of what a public school is like and it brings a real practitioner into the college to teach prospective teachers.

We should also begin to consider just how many "professional education" courses are really necessary in preparing teachers. Some college student who does not "major" in education but who has a solid background in a subject area may be an excellent teacher if the school in which he/she teaches is organized with specific exit standards as advocated in this book. We should seek ways to use these scholars as teachers even if only part time.

We must recognize the intrusive role the federal government has played in teacher preparation programs also. Prestigious universities lead the way in advising the U.S. Department of Education to institute federally funded research which results in specialties in teacher education. We seem to have forgotten what a normal student is. Since we began confusing the terms "average" with "normal" we have accepted a distorted view of abnormality. Normal actually designates a range of ability while average is the arithmetic mean of a series. Most students in our schools are normal although there may not be a true "average" student in the whole school; but when a student varies from the average we begin to think of him/her as abnormal. Thus we have created classes of special students for many youngsters who are well within the range of "normal". Students who vary from the mythical "average" have been over identified so that we now have up to twenty percent of our public school students in some kind of remedial or special education classes. Those students who are really so far from the norm that they do require a special program actually only comprise less than five percent of the total.

If you doubt this, look at a student who has been designated as "attention deficit disordered" because the teacher has some difficulty getting the student to attend to his/her instruction. Put this student in a video arcade and see how long he/she attends to a game. These artificial and harmful designations have proliferated in our schools and teacher training institutions keep adding courses required of teachers for these special classes.

Another influence that has distorted the teacher education programs has been the influence of special interest groups on the federal government, the press and, through funding enticements, to colleges and universities. These special interest groups have "forced" the schools to provide, in addition to what is really needed to function successfully in a student's life such programs as "multi-culturalism", "sex education", "drug abuse prevention", "environmental education", etc. These programs have not proved to be helpful in student learning but they take so much time in indoctrination that teachers have a difficult time teaching students to read and to have enough math skill to interpret for themselves what they want to do about these issues. To review how this pressure has permeated the classroom return to Step One for an example that illustrates how instruction can be distorted.

CONCLUSION

The power of the suggestions in this book can only be realized if parent/s become very familiar with them. The resistance of the traditional school staff will in most cases be resistant to this much change. If the sinking U.S. Public Schools are to be saved we have to recognize that all of the commonly suggested steps for improving education have failed or are failing. Steps like better buildings, smaller class sizes, adding computers, adding guidance counselors and the myriad other conventional changes seem to have only accelerated the decline in education quality. However, they have made advocates of these cosmetic changes feel satisfied that they have done something. These changes do not cause the decline. In fact, most of them would be helpful in improving schooling, but **only if they are undertaken in a school that has first undergone the fundamental change that setting standards for every grade and class calls for.**

One method that has proved useful in some school districts is to get the local school board and school staff to join with parents in reviewing the steps suggested in this book and beginning the cooperative adoption of them. Including media officials in the discussions will be helpful because much public information will be needed to get the community to understand every step as it is being discussed.

Several districts that the author has worked with have published the new student performance standards in the local press and have asked all citizens to look them over to see if there are any standards that they do not want their children to achieve. They were also asked to suggest other standards to be considered by the school.

Because this drastic change will cause teachers to focus in on the set of exit standards and set up individual student records to keep track of which standards have been mastered, it will require considerable time and effort. Parents must be patient and supportive during the change process. Many good teachers have been frustrated by not knowing exactly what they are being held accountable for and will welcome a discrete set of student performance standards whose development they are responsible for. No longer should teacher quality be judged solely by observing them in action or by student popularity. Students' performance after the teacher has "taught" will be the most important criterion by which teacher expertise is judged.

One "red herring" that anyone suggesting these changes for schools will encounter is that this looks like **Outcome Based Education or (OBE).** The controversy pertaining to OBE was really only with the definitions used in describing it. Phyllis Schaffley of Illinois and Bill Spady of Colorado imposed their definitions of OBE and educators were forced into the position of defending a distorted definition of what OBE really is. Outcome based education is practiced in almost every educational or training program in the United States except in public schools and in higher education. Most organizations, including the service academies, set standards for which all are expected to demonstrate mastery.

Bill Spady's definition of OBE was setting standards for what students needed to know and *be like.* It is that latter term which has been rejected by all sensible persons in education because it implies indoctrination of students in all sorts of social issues.. This misunderstanding has been at the root of all the controversy about OBE. I have encountered very few parents who do not want their students to learn the basic skills; when you list these, they are outcomes.

Annual reports comparing the percent of students which are scoring in the highest group one year with the previous year/s percent will be helpful to parents and will result in even the best of schools trying to keep their reports high.

This will also encourage schools where the students have been achieving poorly to show improvement. In the past, when school achievement has been compared school by school, there was little real incentive for the lower ranking school to try harder because it would likely still be in the bottom rankings.

On the following page is an example of 109 Missouri school district records for three years. There were about 5000 students in each grade level reported. These districts were all in some stage of implementing the steps for improvement listed in this book; some farther along than others:

Percent of Students Scoring in Each Quintile on the Missouri Mastery and Achievement Test for Three Years

Year 1—Tests were given statewide. The highest 20% of the scores were placed in the top quintile (HIGH), the next lower 20% in the next lower quintile, etc. You will note how close the 109 districts came to the state average by how near each year 1 quintiles are to 20%

GRADE 3

Read			Math			Science			Social Studies		
Yr.1	Yr.2	Yr.3	Yr.1	Yr.2	Yr.3	Yr.1	Yr.2	Yr.3	Yr.1	Yr.2	Yr.3
23	40	55	25	45	54	24	38	77	27	38	70
21	22	20	19	22	19	21	22	12	21	25	15
18	16	12	19	13	13	19	16	5	17	19	7
18	13	8	17	10	8	17	13	3	16	11	5
29	9	6	20	10	6	19	11	2	19	7	2

GRADE 6

Read			Math			Science			Social Studies		
Yr.1	Yr.2	Yr.3	Yr.1	Yr.2	Yr.3	Yr.1	Yr.2	Yr.3	Yr.1	Yr.2	Yr.3
21	32	46	22	58	62	24	64	71	29	50	50
20	20	23	19	20	16	20	16	20	20	20	18
19	18	14	19	12	9	18	9	6	18	13	12
19	17	12	18	7	6	18	6	3	20	10	10
21	13	5	22	3	7	20	5	0	19	7	10

GRADE 8

Read			Math			Science			Social Studies		
Yr.1	Yr.2	Yr.3	Yr.1	Yr.2	Yr.3	Yr.1	Yr.2	Yr.3	Yr.1	Yr.2	Yr.3
25	45	47	28	60	60	27	59	69	28	50	50
20	23	20	22	17	16	19	17	15	20	20	19
20	15	11	19	11	8	22	11	4	19	13	12
17	11	11	16	8	8	16	6	4	15	9	9
18	6	7	15	4	7	16	7	3	18	8	10

GRADE 10

Read			Math			Science			Social Studies		
Yr.1	Yr.2	Yr.3	Yr.1	Yr.2	Yr.3	Yr.1	Yr.2	Yr.3	Yr.1	Yr.2	Yr.3
24	34	48	25	33	53	25	50	50	24	32	35
21	21	17	21	22	19	21	18	19	21	22	19
18	18	11	19	18	9	19	12	10	19	19	14
19	16	11	15	17	9	17	9	10	18	10	14
18	12	11	18	12	8	18	11	9	18	12	16

Note: You will notice that there were greater gains in the percents of students scoring higher in the lower grades. This may be because the older students had previously experienced difficulty in learning and had not been able to overcome the negative view of school. Also, each year's square represents a different set of students: one can only imagine how much better the students will perform in later years if the progress continues.

As can be seen from the type of reporting on the preceding charts, one can tell what progress, if any, is being made. This report can be done for a single school or for a single classroom to see if learning gains are occurring. In a smaller school or in a single classroom it would be easier to use actual numbers of students in each grade level and subject square instead of percents. There were different students in the tests for each year, but wouldn't you want your child to be in one of the later year's classes? The first column in each square is the first year in which the test was administered and the two following years are shown in the other two columns.

This type of reporting is only appropriate if the test is a *criterion referenced test*. This means that there were at least four or five items for every desired outcome and that mastery was declared only if a student got 3 of 4 or 4 of 5 correct. This is to eliminate the lucky guess but allows for an occasional careless error. In the example given above a different, but equal, form of the test was given each year, so that students didn't just memorize the correct answers from the previous year's test.

Remember that the purpose of teaching for exit standards can not be appropriately assessed using standardized norm-referenced tests which are always designed to *rank* students with each other or some norm and usually results in the "bell-shaped" curve. The purpose of effective teaching is to destroy the bell shaped curve or, at least, skew it far to the right of the "norm."

During your discussions of school reform you will hear a vigorous defense of competition. "Our students will have to compete in the work a-day world; they should get used to it now." There are several false assumptions implied in this statement.

First, schools should be a place to *prepare to compete* successfully at whatever occupation one *chooses*. All youth are in school together, while in adult life they *choose* their competition. Brain-surgeons compete with other brain surgeons, not with bricklayers.

Second, motivation to learn more is not likely to occur if students perceive, over and over again, that they cannot learn as fast as the quickest mind in their class. If, rather, the student is competing with personal past performances, he/she is more likely to continue exerting the effort to do better.

Third, since teacher grades are based on so many different criteria (attendance, deportment, promptness of assignment completion and/or academic performance) they are not usually closely related to future adult job performance standards. School grades and class rank, at present, are not good predictors of the degree of success as adults.

Healthy competition is with one's self; doing better today than yesterday. Competition within industry is between companies and teams within companies. The company or organization which can develop the best teamwork among members of the company will always come out on top.

Being a parent is not easy. Occasionally first time parents believe that life will get easier when the children start school. Actually the duties of parenthood never really end, The quality of schooling a child receives is much more important today than ever before because the world is so much more complex. How to locate and select information in this world of overwhelming available knowledge is critical. If your children do not learn to really comprehend what they read — they have not really learned to read. And all the rest of their school and after-school life they will be handicapped. Even most math problems faced in the real world require accurate reading skill to know what arithmetic function is needed to solve them.

Parents should be partners with the school in helping their children learn at a high level. Calculators and/or computers are great aids but a student should know enough math to immediately perform a mental check to see if the displayed numbers are reasonable. Too many workers today trust the calculator even if it is wildly wrong because they accidentally punched the wrong key or misplaced a decimal point.

The present mysterious gulf that separates the home and the school must be bridged and this can be done by following the steps found in this book. Failure to initiate productive communication on your part may well limit the quality of life for your child.

"It may be that doing our best is not enough; sometimes we have to do what is required"

Winston Churchill

On the opposing page are excerpts of parent reports of student progress. These provide much more meaningful information for parents about their child's achievement than do most "grade cards." The elementary report uses "A" for mastery; "NY" for not yet mastered and, if blank "this objective not tested yet." Secondary students use "I" for non mastery.

If parents, students and teachers are fully informed as to what performance will be required to demonstrate mastery of each listed standard then all will understand precisely where the students are each quarter. Parents can help their child and the student no longer must "guess" what will be required of them as learners. This is only an example; there are many variations possible to do the same thing.

Grade 2

Language Arts Quarter:	1	2	3	4
1. State main idea of a story of passage				
2. Predict outcome of a story				
3. Explain problem & solution in a story or passage				
7. Read and follow two-step directions				
11. Combine sentences with simple conjunction				

Grade 7

Math Quarter:	1	2	3	4
4. Solve linear equations (number sentences)				
6. Compute answer to problem involving percents				
9. Determine reasonable esitmates				
12. Solve problems involving measurement				
14. Construct, read and interpret displays of data				

Grade 9

Science Quarter:	1	2	3	4
3. Identify variables in a specific ecosystem				
6. Identify controls, dependent and independent variables in an experiment				

Grade 10

Social Studies Quarter:	1	2	3	4
5. Explain the role of citixens in the resolution of disputes in the U.S. legal system				
10. Identify major current and historical changes that have led to economic growth over time				
13. List factors that have influenced the development of cultures studied				

EDUCATIONAL INTERNET SITES FOR PARENTS AND TEACHERS

One way parents and teachers can focus children on learning is by using the Internet. Here are a few sites that currently may prove to be helpful: (New sites may be added daily-check a search engine)

1. Air Force new family-friendly site for kids at http://www.af.mil/aflinkjr

2. Berit's "Best Sites for Children" helps you learn about earthquakes, visit the imagination factory and make junk mail jewelry, descend into a volcano, tour a human cell, go on a world safari, solve a crime and fly a kite at h t t p : H d b . c o c h r a n . c o m / d b - HTML:theopage.db

3. Blocking software information from Netparents can be found at http:// www.netparents.org

4. Exploratorium will let you puzzle over opti-

cal illusions, take memory tests and conduct experiments, on line and off at http://www.exploratorium.edu

5. Great Sites for Kids and Parents" from the American Library Association allows pre-school through elementary school children to explore rainbows, black history, castles for kids, news reported by children for children, watch dolphins, learn lullabies and The Kids Web Page Hall of Fame and much more at http://www.ssdesign.coimjparentspage/greatsites/50.htmI

6. The Franklin Institute Science Museum offers on-line exhibits on an array of science and technology topics at http://sin.fi.edu/

7. Global Campfire provides stories and offers links to other good family sites at Parents and Children TogetherOn-line at http://wwwjnddana-edia.ericrec/fl/pcto/menu/htmI

8. Healthlinks provides educational resources through distance learning at http://www. meet. edu/healthlinks/index.html

9. The Jason Project allows you to join an interactive exploration of the oceans, On earth and beyond at http://wwwjasonproject.org

10. Library of Congress provides exhibits on topics ranging from ballet to Jelly Roll Morton, native American flutes to Thomas Jefferson's pasta machine at http://www.loc.gov

11. NASA's Quest Project Site provides adventures in space, including views from the Hubble Space Telescope at http:Hspacelink.nasa.gov

12. Newberry and Calsecott Award Winners can be found at the American Library Association site. This site includes information about authors, Kids Connect (for information on locating information on-line) and educational games at http: //www.ala.org/parents/index.htmI

13. Jean Armour Polly's "100 Great sites in Ten Categories" includes links for kids to art and music, homework help, cartoons and animations, games and toys, reading and writing, science and sports. There are also links for parents and and a section for pre-schoolers at http://www.netmom-com.ikyp.samples/hotlist.htm

14. Steve Savitsky's "Interesting Place for Kids" is an award winning site with many unusual links at http:Hcrc.ricoh.coni/people/steve/kids

BOOKS AND OTHER REFERENCES HELPFUL TO PARENTS AND TEACHERS

•Benson, Galbraith & Espeland, What Kids Need To Succeed. Minneapolis, MN, Free Spirit Publishers, Inc.

•Block, J.J., Efthin, H.E. and Burns, R.B. (1989) Building Effective Mastery Learning Schools. New York, Longman, Inc.

•Bloom, B.S. (1968). Learning for Mastery (UCLA-CSEIP) Evaluation Comment. 1-12

•Bloom, B.S. (1956). Taxonomy of Educational Objectives: The Classification of Educational Goals. New York: Dacid Mckay Co. Inc.

•Cohen, S.A. (1987). Tests: Marked For Life? Ontario, Canada: Scholastic.

•Guskey, T.R. (1997) Implementing Mastery Learning. Belmont, CA: Wasworth.

•Johnson, D. and Johnson, T. (1995) Why violence prevention programs don't work and what does. Educational Leadership. 52(5), 63-68.

•Johnson, D. and Johson, R. (1982) Cooperaton in Learning: Ignored but Powerful. Lyceum, 1982, 5, 22-26, University of Minnesota.

•Levine, D.U. (1987) Improving Student Achievement Through Mastery Learning Programs. San Francisco, Jossey-Bass Publishers.

•Mager, R.F. (1962) Preparing Objectives for Instruction. San Francisco: Fearon Publishers, Inc.

•Sykes, Charles. Dumbing Down Our Kids. New York, NY: St.Martin's Press.

ABOUT THE AUTHOR

Dr. King has had experience at all levels of education, from elementary teacher to graduate professorships at Ohio State Univ. and at Northern Arizona Univ. For 20 years he coordinated curriculum services for the Missouri State Dept. Elem. and Sec. Education. He has been active as an educational speaker in many forums, both nationally and abroad. The author has had numerous articles published in educational journals and has served as editor of two journals. Since 1991 he has served as consultant to school districts in several parts of the U.S. He has presented research papers at national meetings of the National Org for In-Service Education; the ASCD; at the American Educational Research Association; and at The World Congress for School Effectiveness. Most recently he has been a speaker before various parent organizations.